A CASE FOR
Skill

Also by <inline>THE</inline>Life@Work Co.™

A Case for Calling
A Case for Character
A Case for Serving

THE Life@Work Co.™

A CASE FOR
Skill

Discovering the Difference a Godly Man Makes in His Life at Work

DR. THOMAS ADDINGTON & DR. STEPHEN GRAVES

Cornerstone *Alliance*

FAYETTEVILLE, ARKANSAS 72702

Published by Cornerstone Alliance
Post Office Box 1928
Fayetteville, AR 72702

All Scripture quotations, unless otherwise indicated, are taken from the
HOLY BIBLE, NEW INTERNATIONAL VERSION®, NIV®.
Copyright © 1973, 1978, 1984 by International Bible Society. Used by
permission of Zondervan Publishing House. All rights reserved.

Scripture quotations cited as KJV are from the HOLY BIBLE, KING
JAMES VERSION.

ISBN 1-890581-04-6

Cover design by Sean Womack of Cornerstone Alliance.

Printed in the United States of America

1 3 5 7 9 10 8 6 4 2

To our colleagues

*the men and women
of Cornerstone Group
and Cornerstone Alliance*

*Thank you for living out
what this book describes.*

Series Introduction

Our offices are on the fourth floor of the second tallest building in northwest Arkansas. We have an extraordinary view of the rolling hills of Fayetteville from our panoramic picture windows. Although our city is growing, it still has the feel of a small town. Almost everyone knows almost everyone.

From that vantage point we enjoy watching cycles of life unfold around us. Unlike some parts of the country, we benefit from the whole assortment of seasons. The snowy mantle of winter melts into the sweaty heat of summer, with all variations in between.

We also watch the daily routine of hundreds of businesses. At the start of a day we can see the lights of other businesses coming on, like eyes popping open after a good night's sleep. At the end of a day we witness those same lights going out. The next morning it begins all over again. Then again. Then again.

We talk to many men for whom that description sums up their work experience. People come and go; accounts open and close. Creditors get paid; customers get billed. We pick up; we deliver. We punch in; we punch out. The workday begins, then ends. We earn our money; we spend our money. The cycle is unrelenting and unending. Then the cycle quits, and we die.

Is that all there is? Is routine drudgery what a man should expect from his work life and career?

What is the difference in the behavior and experience of a Christian man in his work compared to that of a non-Christian man?

What does it mean to be a Christian who practices dentistry? Does it mean that I have Bible verses on my business card? Do I share Christ with patients while they are under anesthesia? Or perhaps I ought to treat only Christian patients. If someone doesn't pay me, should I send their bill into collections, or should I forgive the debt and maybe pay for it myself? Should I work longer hours to display an incredible work ethic? Or maybe I need to work shorter hours so that I can spend more time with my family or serve on a church or community committee. Do I pay my employees more than the national average? Or do I pay them less so they can learn to live by faith?

What does it mean to be a Christian plumber? Do I cut my rates for Christian customers? Should I work on Sunday, or do I fail to respond to a crisis that comes on the Sabbath? Perhaps I need to hand out gospel tracts to other subcontractors on the job. Should I release one of my crew if he's incompetent? Or are Christians bound to keep every employee on the payroll for life? What does the Bible say about work?

A number of years ago we came across a verse in the New Testament book of Acts that serves as God's final epitaph for King David:

> When David had served God's purpose in his own generation, he fell asleep. (Acts 13:36)

Those words complete a description of David found way back in the Old Testament book of Psalms:

> He chose David his servant and took him from the sheep pens; from tending the sheep he brought him to be the shepherd of his people Jacob, of Israel his inheritance. And David shepherded them with integrity of heart; with skillful hands he led them. (Psalm 78:70-72)

David was a shepherd, a musician, a soldier, and a king. He had a very busy, full, and successful career. We would like to use those verses about David as the basis for exploring the making of a godly man in and through his work world. This short series will consist of four parts:

....David... *served God's purpose...*: A Case for Calling

He chose *David his servant...*: A Case for Serving

....David shepherded them

with *integrity of heart*: A Case for Character

....with *skillful hands* he led them: A Case for Skill

So, we are back to one of our questions from above. Is work basically an unending and unfulfilling cycle of activity? Answer: it depends. On what? On whether or not I know God.

According to King Solomon, one of the wisest and wealthiest men of all time:

A man can do nothing better than to eat and drink and find satisfaction in his work. This too, I see, is from the hand of God.... *To the man who pleases him, God gives wisdom, knowledge and happiness, but to the sinner he gives the task of gathering and storing up wealth to hand*

it over to the one who pleases God. (Ecclesiastes 2:24-26; italics added)

Without God in my life, I might be driven, full of ambition, and very successful. I might even make it to the pinnacle of my profession. But I will not enjoy my work over time. It will not bring me fulfillment. I will be on a treadmill.

These books address a Christian man in the workplace. The definition and clarity that the Bible brings to a man and his work world are reserved for those who enjoy a personal relationship with Jesus. If you don't know Him, we strongly urge you to invite Him into your life. Then join us in exploring the topic of work in the incredibly rich, amazingly untapped pages of Scripture.

> May the favor of the Lord our God rest upon us;
> establish the work of our hands for us—
> yes, establish the work of our hands. (Psalm 90:17)

A word about our writing style. As coauthors, we speak in the first person when telling a story that relates to one of us as individuals. But we do not identify who belongs to which story. To help unravel that mystery, the following are some personal characteristics that will help sort us out.

Steve is an avid fisherman who baited hooks as a young boy on the Mississippi Gulf Coast. His appetite for learning and his energy for making friends have trademarked his twenty-three years of ministry and business.

Tom grew up in Hong Kong as the son of a medical missionary. He spent a number of years driving eighteen-wheelers, and he has taught at three universities.

We live in Fayetteville, Arkansas, love Scripture, and work together as business partners. Our companies and colleagues do work in organizational consulting and publishing. We have a passion to understand biblical principles that apply to work.

Book Introduction

Skill is expected.

Of the four topics considered in this series, calling, serving, character, and skill, we probably know the least about skill. What does Scripture have to say about it?

Quite a bit, as it turns out. Skill is an incredibly rich concept in the Bible, in both the Old and New Testaments. In the Old Testament, God addresses skill directly and specifically with Moses when he is on Mount Sinai to transcribe the Ten Commandments.

One issue becomes very clear through this study. God expects skill in the work of His people. As Christians we do not have the option of mediocrity in our work.

Skill is expected.

Definition of Skill

Understanding something completely
and transforming that knowledge
into creations of wonder
and excellence.

"And David shepherded them with integrity of heart; with skillful hands he led them" (Psalm 78:72).

CONTENTS

CHAPTER ONE

What Is Skill?

Bringing a 540,000-pound Boeing 747 onto the runway at Hong Kong's Kai Tak Airport is one of the ultimate tests of an airline pilot's skill. Professional pilots normally train on simulators that allow them to practice landings at almost every airport. Not so for most pilots flying into Hong Kong. Virtually every airline requires pilots to witness Hong Kong landings from a cockpit jump seat before they are allowed to land an airplane there on their own. According to Cathay Pacific pilot Bob Scott, Kai Tak Airport is as close as you can get in commercial aviation to making an aircraft-carrier landing. A former Royal Navy aircraft-carrier pilot, Scott contends, "If you can land in Hong Kong, then you can land just about anywhere."

Aviation experts maintain that no other final approach in the world is as complicated. The extremely mountainous terrain is supplemented by dense apartment blocks of housing that stretch almost to the very edge of the airport tarmac. The runway extends almost eleven thousand feet straight out into the Hong Kong harbor, on land reclaimed from the Pacific Ocean.

In roughly two minutes the aircraft drops from 1,800 to 675 feet. The landing gear is down, the flaps are extended, and the aircraft is screaming straight into a mountain. All of sudden, while the plane continues to descend, the pilot banks the aircraft as much as thirty degrees to the right in a 4,500-foot turn. Fifteen degrees is the most severe bank most passengers ever experience on a commercial flight. Pilots call it "The Turn." If you are on the right side of the airplane, you are looking directly into apartment windows. In the final thirty seconds of flight the pilot must level the airplane, center it on the runway, and touch down soon enough to avoid running into Victoria Harbor.

Captain Tom Overholt first flew into Hong Kong as a flight engineer on a Northwest Airlines 747. "I was working on the final checks. It was heavy weather; we broke out at just seven hundred feet. By the time I finished my job and swiveled my seat around, I couldn't believe it. I saw this mountain straight ahead and rooftops almost touching the wings. It took my breath away." Overholt calls it "the last real man's ride in the world."[1]

Growing up in Hong Kong, I lived two miles from the end of the runway, directly under the flight path. Landing lights for the final approach were on the roof of the two-story apartment building next to ours. It was against the law to fly kites because they could get tangled in the landing gear. A friend of mine with a good arm claimed he could hit airplanes with baseballs from our roof.

It was an awesome thing to see, hear, and feel those huge jets thunder overhead, just a few hundred feet off the ground. One right after another, they came in only minutes apart. No matter how many thousands I had already seen, I always had to watch the next one. The elite pilots who fly into Hong Kong are very good at what they do.

Skill in action is a wonderful thing to behold:

- A cardiac surgeon who displays confident dexterity in the process of repairing a defective heart valve.
- A professional truck driver who deftly maneuvers a fifty-five-foot eighteen-wheeler into a hard-to-get-to freight dock with only inches of leeway on either side.
- A tenacious salesman who negotiates through almost insurmountable obstacles to close a tough deal.

- A mechanic who finds and fixes a problem that no one else could find or fix.
- An artist who brings life in color out of a blank white canvas.
- A writer who arranges words to make a reader's blood boil, his heart laugh, or his brain think.

When we watch someone accomplish a task with skill, we are amazed. We say such things as "How did you do that?" "That was really something!" "Where did you learn to make that happen?" We love to see skill in action, but what is it exactly? What is skill, really?

The meaning of skill

The Old Testament word for skill comes directly from the Hebrew word *to know*. But this *to know* does not indicate just a superficial understanding of something. It literally means to know completely and thoroughly, so that whatever can be known about something is known. It is the same word used in the King James Version of the Old Testament to describe sexual intimacy between a husband and a wife: "And Adam knew Eve his wife; and she conceived, and bare Cain" (Genesis 4:1, KJV). The word for skill describes knowing something intensely, exhaustively, and entirely. It means leaving nothing unexplored.

As if that were not enough, the definition goes even further. In addition to knowing something completely, skill also indicates the capacity to translate that knowledge into something of great value. According to Scripture, a skillful person is not just someone who has available a huge database of information should someone want to tap it. A person of skill is an individual who has a depth of understanding that is linked to an ability to take that knowledge and turn it into something of significant worth. Skill is often paired with words like *craftsman* and *fine workmanship*.

We attempt to capture the rich biblical meaning of skill as follows:

> Understanding something completely and transforming that knowledge into creations of wonder and excellence.

Frankly, this definition stunned us. We did not realize that Scripture talked much about skill at all, much less with this kind of vibrancy. We sat back from our study and could not help but reflect that the biblical level of skill is far away from where many, if not most, of us are in our work worlds. The implications are enormous.

The usage of skill

Many of the words about skill in the Old Testament were used concerning the building of the tabernacle and the temple. Those two creations were perhaps more important to God then any other in the Old Testament era, apart from the actual work that He was doing in the hearts of His people. The tabernacle and then the temple were the primary dwelling places for God's presence. God was so concerned about the tabernacle's construction that He personally communicated the blueprint details to Moses. After He gave Moses the Ten Commandments, God held the prophet up on Mount Sinai for some additional and rather lengthy instruction, first regarding the furnishings of the tabernacle:

> Make the tabernacle with ten curtains of finely twisted linen and blue, purple and scarlet yarn, with cherubim worked into them by a *skilled craftsman.* (Exodus 26:1; italics added)

And again a few verses later: "Make a curtain of blue, purple and scarlet yarn and finely twisted linen, with cherubim worked into it by a *skilled craftsman*" (Exodus 26:31; italics added).

Then, the focus shifts to the uniform of the priest while he is in the tabernacle: "Tell all the *skilled men* to whom I have given wisdom in such matters that they are to make garments for Aaron, for his consecration, so he may serve me as priest" (Exodus 28:3; italics added). Then, "Fashion a breastpiece for making decisions—the work of a *skilled craftsman*" (Exodus 28:15; italics added)

But the most fascinating reference is the following one, in which God identifies with great precision the craftsmen He has in mind for the project:

Then the Lord said to Moses, "See, I have chosen Bezalel son of Uri, the son of Hur, of the tribe of Judah, and I have filled him with the Spirit of God, with *skill, ability and knowledge in all kinds of crafts*—to make artistic designs for work in gold, silver and bronze, to cut and set stones, to work in wood, and to engage in all kinds of craftsmanship. Moreover, I have appointed Oholiab son of Ahisamach, of the tribe of Dan, to help him. Also *I have given skill to all the crafts-men* to make everything I have commanded you: the

Tent of Meeting, the ark of the Testimony with the atonement cover on it, and all the other furnishings of the tent—the table and its articles, the pure gold lampstand and all its accessories, the altar of incense, the altar of burnt offering and all its utensils, the basin with its stand—and also the woven garments, both the sacred garments for Aaron the priest and the garments for his sons when they serve as priests, and the anointing oil and fragrant incense for the Holy Place. They are to make them just as I commanded you." (Exodus 31:1-11; italics added)

God Himself took such an intense personal interest in setting the standard for skill at the highest level. Of all of the things He chose to talk about up on that mountain with Moses, a significant portion of communication dealt with skilled craftsmen—sometimes by name. God did not have only a passing, casual interest in skill. Far from it—He was directly involved in describing it, identifying it, and giving direction to it.

Throughout Scripture, the word *skill* is applied to a host of different careers, such as writers, traders, musicians, loggers, leaders, weavers, speakers, soldiers, and metalworkers, to mention a few. There can be no question from the usage of the word that skill is very close to the center of God's attention and His heart.

With that in mind, it is not at all surprising that David, a man after God's own heart, was identified by God as a skilled leader. Neither should it be astonishing that Solomon observes in Proverbs: "Do you see a man skilled in his work? He will serve before kings; he will not serve before obscure men" (Proverbs 22:29).

If skill is something worthy of the King's personal attention, then certainly it will be noticed and appreciated by a king.

CHAPTER TWO

Raising the Skill Level

A good friend of ours worked for years in a Fortune 50 company. Mike (not his real name) signed on as a young college graduate and moved up through the ranks rather quickly. He was skilled in information systems as well as marketing, and he held a variety of assignments as his career progressed. Mike worked for five years before he met a Christian who was known in the company for his level of skill.

Until he met another Christian (we will call him Todd), Mike did not advertise widely that he was a follower of Jesus. Why? Because he was afraid of persecution? No. Because he was ashamed to be identified with Christ? No. Because as a whole, his Christian coworkers did not distinguish themselves with high levels of competence.

The Christians in the organization had a great reputation for showing stellar character and for being wonderful servants. They had Scripture verses on their desks. They conducted Bibles studies during lunch breaks. They helped colleagues navigate personal problems. They did not steal company technology or cash. They were very open about their faith. Everybody trusted them. And it was not so much that they were bad at what they did. They just were not very good at what they did.

But Mike kept hearing about Todd. Todd was an aggressive Christian. No one who worked with and for him was uncertain about Whom he served and what he believed. But make no mistake. He was also at the top of his game. In an extremely competitive corporate environment, this man was viewed both inside and outside the company as one of the best in the world at what he did. He was on the cutting edge of a technology that he had helped develop and that he continued to improve. He often received calls from top executives of noncompeting companies around the world who wanted to learn from him. In one case we know about, a board chairman flew his entire board on two corporate Gulfstream IVs to spend two days with Todd.

Like loads of other folks in the company, Mike wanted to work for Todd. So he kept putting in for assignments to work with this fellow and eventually was transferred to the team that Todd led. For Mike, it was like a cup of cool water on a hot day—to work for an overt Christian who was extraordinarily skilled at what he did. That man became Mike's mentor and still occupies that role today.

God's definition of skill raises the standard.

The definition of skill that comes out of Scripture is worlds away from work defined by mediocrity. Skill in the Bible is not the characteristic of someone who says, "I guess I know enough to get by" or "I suppose I'm doing an OK job because I'm still receiving a paycheck." A person of skill does not excuse his mediocre work with such words as "I've been here twenty-five years, so I ought to get some respect from people around here." The skill of Scripture is the kind of quality that knows something better, understands something more thoroughly, and translates something more completely into a creation of unique worth than anything else could.

Our ultimate example of skill is embodied in the life that Jesus lived on this earth. He healed in cases where no other physician could make disease go away. He was persuasive even with Pharisees and doctors of the law, who had an obvious agenda to get rid of Him. Jesus mentored His disciples so well that after His ascension into heaven they took the Good News around the world. There was virtually nothing Jesus did during the three-plus years of His full-time ministry that did not demonstrate great skill.

But He also was very skilled as a carpenter before those years of full-time ministry. The word used to describe Jesus in Mark 6:3 is the Greek word *tekton*. As William Barclay notes, "A *tekton* was more than a carpenter; he was a craftsman who could build a wall or a house, construct a boat, or make a table or a chair, or throw a bridge across a little stream."[1] Even before He was publicly identified as the Messiah, Jesus was known as a skilled craftsman. *Tekton* pictures someone who, with a minimum of technical equipment and a maximum of craftsmanship, could make something of beauty out of very little.

In many of the older cities of Europe it was common for craftsmen to hang a sign outside their shop that indicated their trade and their slogan. It was the same in Israel during New Testament times. In Matthew 11:30, Jesus commented that His yoke is easy. The Greek word for *easy* means "well-fitting." Perhaps the sign that hung above the door of His carpenter's shop in Nazareth was in the form of an ox yoke with the words "My yokes fit well" inscribed on it.[2]

SPEED VS. QUALITY

Sometime during the Industrial Revolution a subtle shift began to take place in the crafts. Speed and uniformity eventually became more important than quality and craftsmanship. A craftsman was someone who understood his specific craft from start to finish. The advent of the assembly line divided the process of making something into small parts. An assembly-line worker does not know and understand the entire creation process for a product. He only knows his small fragment.

It has only been in the last few years that the spotlight has turned back to quality. The Total Quality movement attempts to take a craftsmanlike approach within the context of high-speed manufacturing. Zero defects is the goal—proper engineering before the process begins. Every worker in the process becomes responsible for the quality of the final product. Inspection of raw materials occurs on the front end instead of inspection of finished product on the back end.

We do not at all suggest that the Industrial Revolution, the assembly line, and all the progress they have contributed are bad. But we do know this for sure: Regardless of the context of my work, the Bible makes it clear that I am to bring skill to the task. I bring a craftsman's eye and intensity to what I am doing.

I can do that in any environment, even if it is not expected or rewarded.

CREDENTIALS VS. COMPETENCE

We love credentials. Degrees. Certifications. Awards. Undergraduate education. Graduate school. Postgraduate work. They may all be part of contributing to a person's level of skill. But they are not the same thing as skill. And in some cases they do not bring much to the table at all.

According to Scripture, skill consists of a combination of

1. Raw ability, which comes directly from God;
2. Filling by the Holy Spirit in specific relation to the task He wants me to accomplish; and
3. Experience, education, and maturity in combination with each other.

When I taught at the university, students often came to me and asked if I thought they ought to continue for more advanced degrees. After we sat down and mapped out what they wanted to accomplish once they left the academic environment, it was often clear whether or not more education would be helpful. In many cases it was. In at least as many situations, however, an additional credential probably would not have been helpful.

Credentials do not by themselves create a skilled man. They can, however, be part of an indispensable package that aids him in becoming a man of skill.

So if I'm a Christian, how should I look on the job? Do I have an option to be mediocre? Is it OK just to be OK? Should I be happy with a slightly above average performance review? Should I be content to let other people in the company carry the brunt of being able to make things happen?

Obviously not. Scripture sets a higher standard for my competence level at work than anything else we have ever been exposed to. As a Christian in the workplace, I ought to have an insatiable curiosity to learn what I need to know to understand my work thoroughly and to the core. There should be no question around the office, on the job, or in the company about my level of skill.

The word *Christian* should be synonymous with words like *wonder* and *excellence*.

The Holy Spirit lifts our level of skill.

I understand the Holy Spirit's role in calling. How can I know my calling unless He communicates it to me? I understand the Holy Spirit's role in character. It is virtually impossible to develop godly character without the Holy Spirit. I also understand the Holy Spirit's role in serving. How can I learn how to be a good servant without His help in my life?

But what is the Holy Spirit's role in skill? Far more significant that any of us might have thought.

As we mentioned before, while Moses was up on the mountain receiving the Ten Commandments and other instructions directly from the mouth of God, one of the most surprising things God said related to specific men and their skill. God identified Bezalel as a skilled man whom He wanted directly involved in the tabernacle project. That by itself is amazing. But there is more to the equation in this case. Bezalel was not only specifically chosen by God for a task, the man was also filled with the Holy Spirit for that task: "I have chosen Bezalel... and I have filled him with the Spirit of God... for work" (Exodus 31:2-4).

Bezalel as a skilled craftsman was personally appointed by God. Then he was filled with the Holy Spirit specifically as a supplement to his skill as a craftsman, for the purpose of his work.

Moses then confirmed that combination of skill and God's Spirit when announcing Bezalel's appointment to the nation of Israel in Exodus 35.

Then Moses said to the Israelites, "See, the Lord has chosen Bezalel son of Uri, the son of Hur, of the tribe of Judah, and he *has filled him with the Spirit of God,* with skill, ability and knowledge in all kinds of crafts—to make artistic designs for work in gold, silver and bronze, to cut and set stones, *to work* in wood and to engage in all kinds of artistic craftsmanship." (Exodus 35:30-33; italics added)

But Bezalel is far from unique. Later as Moses was struggling to accomplish all his duties as leader of God's people, the Holy Spirit was given to a group of men designated to help him. Moses did not have time to arbitrate between all the disputes of the Israelite nation. So he appointed seventy elders who could judge the easier cases and leave only the most difficult ones for himself. As that responsibility was given to the elders:

The Lord said to Moses: "Bring me seventy of Israel's elders who are known to you as leaders and officials among the people. Have them come to the Tent of Meeting, that they may stand there with you. I will come down and speak with you there, and I will take of the Spirit that is on you and put the Spirit on them. They will help you carry the burden of the people so that you will not have to carry it alone." (Numbers 11:16-17)

In the book of Judges, there is a whole string of leaders for whom the Holy Spirit and their call to a specific work task came simultaneously:

- Othniel in Judges 3:10;
- Gideon in Judges 6:34;
- Jephthah in Judges 11:29; and
- Samson in Judges 13:25.

David was filled with God's Spirit at the time of his anointing as king of Israel in 1 Samuel 16:13.

In the New Testament the disciples were given the task of carrying the gospel all over the world. That great commission was specifically linked with the coming of the Holy Spirit to help them fulfill that task: "But you will receive power when the Holy Spirit comes on you; and you will be my witnesses in

Jerusalem, and in all Judea and Samaria, and to the ends of the earth" (Acts 1:8).

Those are just a few examples from Scripture that link the work that we are to do and the filling that the Holy Spirit gives us. Our passion for Jesus and the role of the Holy Spirit in our lives are not limited only to being a "great dad." Or developing our character. Or even staying sexually pure. Our passion for Jesus is just as relevant and just as necessary when it comes to the skill that we bring to our work.

The work of the Holy Spirit in our work life is a crucial distinguishing mark in accomplishing tasks on the job. The non-Christian has raw ability that God gives. The non-Christian also has the benefit of education, experience, and maturity. But the non-Christian does not have the Spirit of God as part of his work equation. One out of three very important ingredients is missing. The Holy Spirit plays an indispensable role in lifting our level of skill.

CHAPTER THREE

Getting Focused

B ill McCartney, cofounder of Promise Keepers, is as focused a man as we have ever met. He is intense. He is passionate. There is very little he does not observe. When you have a conversation with him, he looks right through you and goes to the core. There is not much small talk with Coach.

Part of that is a result of his personality. That is the kind of guy he is. We did not know him when he was a college football coach, but his players would probably describe him in somewhat the same way.

But there is more to his focus than just his personality. He is in a second career. Among other things, that means he is developing a new set of skills that relate specifically to God's new calling on his life.

As CEO of Promise Keepers, he is constantly pulled in different directions and into diverse situations, both from inside and outside the organization. But he will not allow himself to be pulled anywhere that does not conform to the skill set that God has given him and that he is developing. At the same time, he is drawn like a magnet to areas to which he feels called and which are aligned with his skill.

Focus. You just do not meet great leaders who have a scattered focus. Good leaders know what they are all about. They concentrate in areas where their skills are best utilized and where those skills shine.

That strategy and orientation come right out of Scripture.

Developing skill requires focus.

Solomon. When Solomon took over the throne from his father, David, as the king of Israel, he spent some quiet time with God. Solomon had already established that he would follow in the footsteps of his father, David. According to the text, he showed his love for God by walking according to the statutes his father had lived by.

During an encounter with God at the very beginning of Solomon's reign, God appeared to him and told him to ask for whatever he wanted God to give him. Solomon responded very simply: "Give your servant a discerning heart to govern your people and to distinguish between right and wrong" (1 Kings 3:9).

Just one focused sentence of request! Solomon didn't have a grocery list. As a young king, burdened with the kinds of judgments and decisions that he would have to make, he focused on a specific kind of skill that would make him a good king.

To this day, Solomon is known as a wise man. According to Scripture, he was the wisest man who ever lived, except for Jesus Christ. The Old Testament books that he authored, Song of Solomon and Proverbs, are referred to as "wisdom literature."

If you had gone to Solomon and asked the question, "What skill do you need to develop in order to do your job well?" he could have answered on the spot, "I need a discerning heart to govern my people and to distinguish between right and wrong." For Solomon, his entire ability to govern well came down to that one statement. He could articulate it; he focused on it; he wrote about it; and he asked God for it. It is the skill that distinguished him from other kings.

Solomon's skill in these matters did not come entirely with one sweep of God's hand over him. The fact that Solomon had skill implied that he had been a diligent student of God's Word, of nature, of his father's method of ruling the kingdom, and of other disciplines of learning. God does not seem to endow someone with skills who is not actively pursuing them on a natural plane.

Developing an exceptionally focused sense of what I do does not mean that I cannot have a wide range of interests. Look at Solomon. He was an incredible businessman. Scripture contends that Solomon was wealthier than any man who has ever lived before or since. He could negotiate, and he could trade. Furthermore, he understood a wide range of knowledge beyond governing. Ecclesiastes discourses about pleasure and work, leadership and knowledge, as well as wisdom. The range of subjects that Solomon writes about in Proverbs is truly remarkable.

Paul. In much the same way as Solomon, Paul brought a focused skill to his work. We know precisely what his calling was. God told Ananias, "This man [Paul] is my chosen instrument to carry my name before the Gentiles and their kings and before the people of Israel" (Acts 9:15). Paul himself confirmed that calling when he reported to the Galatians what the apostles had concluded about his mission: "They saw that I had been entrusted with the task of preaching the gospel to the Gentiles, just as Peter had been to the Jews" (Galatians 2:7).

We also know that Paul was filled with the Holy Spirit when Ananias laid hands on him. But what was the focus of his skill?

Paul developed a magnificent skill in communicating Christ persuasively in multiple contexts and cultures. Consider some examples:

- *To Jewish Christians.* The Jerusalem Council, which is described in Acts 15, dealt with a volatile issue that was very traumatic to the early church. Should Gentile believers be required to undergo circumcision? Paul, along with Peter, Barnabas, and James, convinced the apostles and elders not to place that added burden on new Gentile believers.

- *To Greek philosophers.* Acts 17 records one of the most complete and remarkable speeches in all the Bible. Paul grabbed an opportunity to speak to a group of Epicurean and Stoic philosophers at the Areopagus, which was their place of discussion and debate. He presented the gospel, using their own beliefs and persuasive communication techniques to his advantage. He knew the Greek culture and its prevailing thought so well that some of the philosophers who listened actually became followers of Christ.

- *To local churches.* Paul planted churches and spoke in more than thirty locations across Palestine, Asia, Macedonia, and Italy. He also wrote a series of letters, which we still enjoy as thirteen of our New Testament books.

- *To Roman rulers.* Paul was able to convey the gospel message to Felix, Festus, and King Agrippa, and perhaps even to Caesar himself.

Paul had many interests and was highly skilled and educated. His skill focus, however, was quite simple. Whether in written or spoken form, he wanted to be effectively communicating the gospel. The contexts varied widely, from riots in Jerusalem to a palace in Rome. The cultures he communicated in were also diverse. But the focus of his skill was very precise.

Developing skill requires an exceptionally focused sense of what I do.

CHAPTER FOUR

Skill and Success

There are many stories of skillful men who zoom up the career ladder of success. Those men live in the books of the Bible and on the pages of the *Wall Street Journal.* It makes sense to us when skill and success end up partnering with each other.

Then there are the cases where men of mediocre skill face career stall-outs. Someone else is promoted, positions are eliminated, and functions are outsourced. Again, we can understand that scenario. It can be explained and understood.

But then there are other accounts, stories that also appear in Scripture and in the lives of men we all know. Sometimes men of genuine skill do not live in the glow of a successful career. What their skill ought to deliver somehow eludes them. They work hard and well, and little career good happens. That is not an uncommon happening.

We need to make one more point before we draw our study of skill to a conclusion:

Working skillfully does not guarantee success.

If David had written a resume, this is what it would have looked like on his thirtieth birthday:

David, son of Jesse
120 Goliath Falls Trail
Jerusalem, Israel

BIOGRAPHICAL DATA

Born in Bethlehem to Jesse as the youngest of eight children. Married to Michal, daughter of Saul, king of Israel.

WORK EXPERIENCE

Shepherd; Bethlehem
Responsibilities included taking care of my father's sheep and rescuing sheep from jaws of lions and bears. I also wrestled with lions and bears and killed them. Anointed king of Israel by Samuel the prophet.

Musician to the royal court; Jerusalem
Responsibilities included playing the harp for King
Saul, especially when he was under significant
pressure. Began part-time; went to full-time
employment at the king's specific request.

Shepherd, messenger; Socoh in Judah and Bethlehem
Responsibilities included taking care of my father's
sheep, as well as carrying messages and supplies to
and from my father in Bethlehem and brothers
fighting the Philistines under the command of
King Saul. Accomplishments included killing the
Philistine giant Goliath, who had defied both the
Israelite army and God.

*High-ranking army officer, musician to the royal
court;* Jerusalem
Responsibilities included playing the harp for King
Saul when depressed. Also led military campaigns
against the various enemies of Israel.
Accomplishments included moving quickly up in
rank as I led the troops successfully through many
battles. Won constant recognition from fellow officers and soldiers, as well as the general public. Was

credited with more success than all the rest of Saul's officers. Reason for leaving: philosophical differences with employer, King Saul.

REFERENCES

Jonathan, son of Saul, king of Israel
Samuel, prophet of God

Notice the pattern evidenced by David's resume. He began in a relatively humble position as a shepherd, worked slowly into a significant job in the king's court, and shot to top of the mountain. What the resume fails to mention is that he soon fell off a cliff. Just when he was supposed to be getting into the stride of his career, near his thirtieth birthday, he became a fugitive running from the death penalty.

A more forthcoming resume would have included this entry:

Fugitive; Judah and Philistine
Responsibilities included trying to stay alive on the run while being pursued by King Saul and his army. Spent years camping out in the wilderness and living in caves. Supported myself by organizing raiding parties against Philistines, while at

other times joining the Philistines in raids against their enemies.

According to the text, David was very skilled at what he did. Furthermore, we know beyond a shadow of a doubt that he was called and anointed to be king of Israel. However in the middle of that calling and in the center of that evidence skill, he experienced anything but career success.

We need to be cautioned against thinking that if we perform our job skillfully we will automatically experience career success. Scripture makes no such promise. Many other things come into play as God fulfills His purpose and as we live out our calling. Success as the world defines it may or may not be one of the results. That, however, does not diminish our need and responsibility to perform our work with a high level of skill. God's definition of skill is still true and is still relevant even if it does not guarantee our career success.

CHAPTER FIVE

What Skill Looks Like

We are committed in this short series to offering real-life examples of the topic under discussion and scrutiny. In this chapter you will meet three men who live out what it means to be a skilled worker. They come from different walks of life.

Mickey Rapier is a musician and worship leader at Fellowship Bible Church in northwest Arkansas. He is one of our pastors and an exceptionally gifted man.

Ken Larson is the CEO of Slumberland, a chain of home-furnishings stores in the Midwest that is headquartered in St. Paul, Minnesota. We have always thought of Ken as an extraordinary entrepreneur.

Fitz Hill is a coach for the Arkansas Razorbacks.

The worship leader: Mickey Rapier

Mickey Rapier isn't the type to live in clutter, so he keeps the closet door closed. This otherwise highly organized worship pastor doesn't use a computer or even a filing cabinet to compartmentalize the thousands of items he has collected for possible use during a Sunday service.

Instead, he uses the closet. Behind its closed door is the world of Mickey Rapier—stacks and stacks of music, notes, letters, and articles; anything he has come across and thought someday might apply to some message. There is a stack for Christmas and a stack for Easter. There are stacks for just about every other holiday or topic that might come up, and each stack grows by the day.

But the stacks are more than a practical mechanism for storing information. They are symbolic as well. They represent the core method Mickey uses to take his God-given talents and turn them into "creations of wonder and excellence." They represent how Mickey attacks every task he values—with a passion for learning as much as he can even if he might never use 99 percent of what he comes to know.

Mickey realized as a high school student that his passion for music and singing wouldn't develop without training, which he couldn't get in his rural community. But he wanted to sing. Ever since he heard the visiting music leader at his church's revival meeting, Mickey knew he wanted to sing. And it was beginning to dawn on him that singing was something he could give to God. He loved the competition of athletics, but he knew he could never play college ball, much less make a living in sports. He decided to sing for a living and use his gift for God.

But as a high school senior, he wasn't ready for Nashville, and he knew it. So he went to college on scholarship as a tuba player. And after overcoming an initial fear of performing before the university faculty, he earned a scholarship as a vocalist.

The more his teachers helped him develop his particular talents as a singer—primarily a French baritone voice that is as rich and delightful as your favorite hot-fudge dessert—the more he was eager to spend time practicing the craft. And the more he worked on his musical skills, the more he came to appreciate the skills of others. Even though he knew he would never sing opera, he wanted to study it. And the same held true for most other styles.

He began to study anything he could find about musicians, songwriters, and singers, with a particular leaning toward finding out what people were thinking when they wrote their songs. He was searching for the meaning, good or bad, behind the words and notes.

Mickey was also (and is) a student of people as well as words. He soaks in everything he sees in others. When they succeed, he wants to know why so he can imitate their methods. When they fail, he wants to know what went wrong so he can avoid it or correct it if he is ever in a similar situation. In college, he directed a small ensemble that traveled from church to church singing and sharing testimonies. He fell in love with the girl who would become his wife and the thrill of seeing people respond to the gospel.

His first church job was a part-time position he held while still in college. The senior pastor was a true shepherd to the people of his congregation, and he worked tirelessly and selflessly to meet their needs. From him, Mickey began to refine his work ethic.

After leaving college, Mickey was full of energy and ready to set the world ablaze—starting with his first church—with new ideas. But the senior pastor there helped him harness that passion with patience, and Mickey came to understand the value of taking baby steps when those around him weren't ready to run.

His creative skills were developed largely at his next stop, a small church where the pastor had been a seventeen-year missionary to Japan. The pastor's time abroad made him open to new ideas, and he encouraged Mickey to be creative when organizing the services. When Mickey had a new idea, this pastor's response would be "Go for it." Once again, Mickey found himself deep in study, reading and listening to as much as possible in hopes of finding the perfect song or anecdote to fit the topic of the pastor's upcoming sermon. And with this pastor, a whole new world of modern Christian music was available to go along with the classics.

Mickey's next assignment was as leader of the college ministry in a large church near the campus of a state university. There his skills for administration were refined. No longer was he working with a congregation of two hundred, but a student population of twice that. He soon learned to "think big" and to delegate tasks to others either because they were better at those tasks or because he simply didn't have time to do it all. Administrative skills, which aptitude tests would later reveal he possessed, suddenly began to take shape.

Each stop along the way helped prepare Mickey for his current job as worship leader at a large regional church, where he is in charge of organizing and planning each week's worship celebration so that the songs, the teaching, the music, and all of the other tools he can come up with work together to drive home the theme of the day.

There is one other factor Mickey uses in developing the skills he needs for that job, one that works together with the self-study, the study of others, and the practice of mentoring. He calls it "the train wreck" factor. Every time Mickey wrecks the train—and sometimes he's the only one who notices that it has derailed—he finds something that makes future rides smoother. Each trip to the stage teaches something new about what audiences will respond to and what turns them off.

It is really trial and error. But it is trial and error with a focus. There is a point to the weeks upon weeks of planning with his staff, to the days upon days of practicing and memorizing, to the nights upon nights of reading, to the hours upon hours of listening to new music, and to the endless creative leaps he and his worship team take in front of thousands of worshipers.

It all fits with Mickey's passion for worship and his calling from God. And it gives him something to do with all the stuff in his closet.

The entrepreneur: Ken Larson

Ken Larson was busy turning a small bedding company into a regional home-furnishings giant when he learned a huge lesson about motives.

A manufacturer had called one day to say that it was yielding to pressure from one of Ken's competitors and that Ken's Slumberland stores could no longer sell its product line.

So after a great deal of thought and consultation with friends, Ken decided to take legal action against both the competitor and the manufacturer. It was the right thing to do, he decided, and he was doing it for all the right reasons.

The system soon bore that out. Before the matter got to court, both parties agreed to settle. So Ken was feeling pretty good as he sat down in his attorney's office to sign the victory papers. But there was one paper Ken didn't count on signing—a confidentiality agreement.

Ken was devastated. He never thought he would have to sign something agreeing to keep the terms of the settlement a secret. But when that document was placed in front of him, Ken immediately came face-to-face with one of his primary motives behind taking the problem into the legal system. He wanted the community and the industry to know he had won. And the fact that he was in the right was more coincidental than he wanted to admit.

What God taught Ken that day was the importance of truly understanding his real motives. It has been an ongoing and difficult learning process for Ken, and he doesn't always like the answers he finds. But he strongly believes that once he understands his real motives, he has a much better chance of getting done what he wants to get done. And ultimately, the motives are more important to God than the numbers in a bank account.

Why is that relevant to developing skill? Understanding what motivates himself and those around him has been a key skill in Ken's success as an entrepreneur. It has been a central factor in his ability to build a home-furnishing empire that has grown to forty-six franchises and corporate stores in six different states.

There are other skills, of course, necessary to become a successful businessman. For Ken, some of the skill sets have changed as he has matured. Others have remained constant. The skills Ken finds important include:

- The ability to transition from one season of life to another. Ken isn't the same person he was fifteen or twenty years ago, and neither is his job. He went from being a manager who did everything to becoming a manager who delegated to others to becoming a CEO. The ability to adapt to the changes in his own personality, to the changes in his corporate world, and to the changes in his industry not only has helped keep Ken's company from growing stale, it's kept it on the cutting edge.

- The ability to trust and show confidence in those around you. Even though Ken has hundreds of employees, his day-to-day work requires him to relate to a relatively small group of key people. Those people must know Ken believes in them. It is something he can't fake. They know when he's not buying what they are selling or when he is losing confidence.

- The ability to listen and understand what others are communicating. Ken can't just sit quietly and nod his head when employees, customers, and vendors talk. He has to honestly understand what they mean in order to make the most of the information they have.

- The ability to value other people. As a matter of policy, Slumberland values other people. It is the VOP (Value of the Person) policy, and it starts at the top. Ken believes everyone in the company, from the top to the bottom, must show love, dignity, and respect for customers and coworkers.

• The ability to hire motivated people and then to keep them motivated. One of the ways he does that is with a psychological assessment. Every potential manager takes the test so that Ken will have an idea about what motivates the person, what the person's interest in the company is, and how the person will fit into the company culture.

The thread that runs through the entire fabric, though, is motivation—the empowering force that is derived from one's motives. Ken believes the key to success in any line of work is the ability to sell ideas. And the key to selling anything is motivation.

Developing such motivation from within requires more than coming up with ideas, but that is the first step. It requires developing a clear picture of what needs to be achieved. And for a leader of a company, it requires effectively translating those goals to a broader group of people.

Motivation is what separates the daydreamers from the achievers. It is the action screaming out more loudly than the words.

Defining a goal isn't always easy, but Ken has come to understand that there has to be a target. That target can change when circumstances change, but it can't fade away. When an employee loses sight of the target, his motivation soon disappears as well. People with nothing to shoot for seldom hit anything of value. That is why Ken believes the most powerful combination in an employee is when the individual's personal objective lines up with the corporate objective.

The coach: Fitz Hill

Fitz Hill was in junior high school when he began refining the primary skill he would need for his career, even though he had no idea what he would do with his life or that what he was doing at the time would help make him good at it.

In fact, the skill Fitz Hill began learning then, and cherishes so dearly now, probably isn't one most people would associate with Hill's job as an assistant football coach at the University of Arkansas.

Football coaches are part salesman, part tactician, part teacher. To succeed, they must develop the ability to recruit and motivate good players. They must develop the ability to create a winning game plan. And they must develop the ability to train the members on the team.

They work twelve to fifteen hours a day during the season, watching film to find the smallest of weaknesses in their opponents, calling prospects who may never even visit the campus, much less play for the team, meeting with other members of the staff, meeting with the players, and, eventually, coaching the players.

But to Hill, those are all secondary skills.

The primary skill, the one that has become part of his second nature and the one that weaves its way through all the others, is the skill of influence.

The world, including his employers, may measure Hill's performance based on how many passes the receivers catch, how many touchdowns the offense scores, and how many wins the team posts. But Hill's measuring stick has one primary mark: how many lives he influences.

For Hill, the only thing he can take with him when he dies is his influence.

So while Hill was thrilled to see J. J. Meadors become the school's all-time leading receiver, he was more elated when Meadors phoned a year later to say he had completed his degree and gotten a job.

Hill had developed a relationship and made an impact.

Hill began learning his people skills when he was running for school offices. From the eighth grade through his senior year, Hill was elected president of either the student body or the student council.

It wasn't an easy task for an African American in a school that was 70 percent white. Hill knew he had to get the white vote without losing the African American vote. He needed friends from both races, so he began developing relationships.

But he had no idea he would be using those skills as a football coach. Hill played football in college, but he planned to be a journalist. He was working on those skills at Ouachita Baptist University when a family crisis changed his career track. Six weeks after his father lost a three-year-long battle with cancer, Hill's mother had a stroke that left her requiring twenty-four-hour care (to this day). Hill lived at home, cared for his mother, played football, and went to college for a semester until an aunt in California agreed to take in his mother.

It was during a 1984 Christmas trip to California to see his mother that Hill popped a cassette tape into his car stereo. He wasn't really interested in the tape, but a friend had given it to him. What else was he going to listen to while driving across the desert? So Hill listened as Grant Taft, then the head football coach at Baylor University, talked about coaching.

"Preachers, teachers, bankers—they have influence on people," Taft said. "But nobody has influence on people like a coach. A coach gets a kid's attention."

On that drive across the desert, Hill discovered his calling. He wanted to have the type of positive influence on kids that his parents had had on him. So instead of writing for the college newspaper, he spent his final two years of college writing head coaches all across the country in search of a job as a graduate assistant coach. He landed a spot at Northwestern (La.) State, then at Arkansas. The job at Arkansas soon turned into a full-time position.

Now Hill is busy coaching—and influencing.

When he first began coaching, Hill realized the true impact he could have on young athletes, especially other African Americans. Anything he told them to do, they did. He had a position of authority, and they immediately respected the position. The more time he spent around them, the more they learned to respect him as a person.

Hill was grateful for the twenty years he had had his parents, and he realized most of the African American kids he was coaching didn't have the advantage of such a strong and stable family. He was determined to fill in the gaps. So he began working on ways to develop trust and build relationships.

The political skills he learned early on were good, but he needed more. Hill has taken several approaches to refining his skills so that he can effectively lead young men.

For starters, he works hard to be sensitive to the needs of minorities. When he travels around the country to recruit players, be it the inner city or rural farmland, he really checks out the surroundings and tries to put himself in that environment. Hill comes from a good family and a good home, and now he makes a good living. But he refuses to look down on anyone who has less. He keeps in mind that our experiences shape our perspectives, and he tries to understand the perspectives of the young people he is contacting.

Hill likes to think of it as a camera lens. "Too many people," he says, "won't take the time to change the lens and look at things differently."

The older he gets, the more Hill has to work at learning and understanding what he sees when he switches to the lens of an eighteen-year-old. He works on that by staying in touch. In the off-season, when he doesn't have to yell and scream at his players, he invites them to his home for regular visits, and he drops by the apartment complex where most of the players live at least twice a week.

He listens to their music and watches their television shows, even when he doesn't always care for what he is hearing or seeing. And he listens closely to whatever they have to say.

When Hill was still a graduate assistant, his National Guard army-reserve unit was called to duty in Desert Storm. Hill's understanding of trust was heightened. Once the troops developed a trust in their leader, they were willing to die for him—just like Jesus died for us. Only after developing that trust can the leader exert his influence. Hill tries to develop the trust with his players first so that he can be in a position to influence their lifestyles.

Hill also has continued his formal education. In earning his master's degree in student personnel services and in working on his doctorate in education leadership, Hill has taken fifteen hours in counseling courses so that he can better understand what he sees and hears when he deals with his athletes.

When he completes his doctorate, Hill could switch career paths and no doubt rise quickly into a position as an administrator in an ivory-tower school. But he has no desire to do that. He wants to stay in the trenches, dealing with kids and their problems. The way he sees it, being a coach at a major college opens doors for him—doors into the homes of young people and doors into the offices of people who can help make social changes. And his higher education will lend credibility to the programs and solutions he devises.

It is just one more step in improving the skill he first began to develop way back in the eighth grade—the skill of influence.

Conclusion

How can we sum up?

We were not sure where this study of skill would take us when we began. We have learned much that we did not know before. We now understand that Scripture defines skill very specifically. And that God Himself cares about the level of skill that His children display in their work. That the Holy Spirit is integral to our developing skill in our work.

But at the end of the study we are left with one unescapable feeling that helps put it all in perspective. For the Christian, skillful work is a form of worship to God. The raw ability itself comes from Him. He is intimately involved in its maturity through the Holy Spirit. And He brings us opportunities for learning, education, and experience to fine-tune it even further.

Skill is worship, just like developing godly character, knowing and living our calling, and serving.

"Bless all his skills, O Lord, and be pleased with the work of his hands" (Deuteronomy 33:11).

Where Do I Go from Here?

1. *Define your skill.*

   It is impossible to develop something that cannot be defined. We recommend that you actually write down, in a couple of sentences or a paragraph, what your skill is. Take your time and be precise.

2. *Determine a plan for developing it.*

   Developing skill is a process, not an event. In fact, it most likely is a lifelong quest. How will it be developed? What are the steps? If it is impossible to lay out the entire plan, what are the obvious next steps?

3. *Become very intentional in praying for it.*

   As is clear from this study, the Holy Spirit is absolutely crucial to our skill development. The skill that you carefully defined above needs to be offered back to God. It is He who gave it to you; it is on His behalf that you exercise it. Ask Him to help you develop and evidence it to its fullness.

Notes

Chapter One

1. Peter S. Greenberg, "Dead-on landing demand makes Hong Kong flight last wild ride," *Los Angeles Times Syndicate*, as reported in the *Arkansas Democrat-Gazette*, 26 January 1997.

Chapter Two

1. William Barclay, *The Mind of Jesus* (New York: Harper & Row, 1960), p. 9.
2. Ibid.

If you liked this book and would like to know more about ^{THE}Life@Work Co.™ or Cornerstone, please call us at 1-800-739-7863.

Other ways to reach us:

Mail: Post Office Box 1928
            Fayetteville, AR 72702

Fax: (501) 443-4125

E-mail: LifeWork@CornerstoneCo.com

A CASE FOR
Calling

Also by <small>THE</small> Life@Work Co.™

A Case for Character
A Case for Skill
A Case for Serving

A CASE FOR
Calling

Discovering the Difference a Godly Man Makes in His Life at Work

DR. THOMAS ADDINGTON & DR. STEPHEN GRAVES

Cornerstone *Alliance*

FAYETTEVILLE, ARKANSAS 72702

Published by Cornerstone Alliance
Post Office Box 1928
Fayetteville, AR 72702

ISBN 1-890581-01-1

Cover design by Sean Womack of Cornerstone Alliance.

Printed in the United States of America

1 3 5 7 9 10 8 6 4 2

To our parents

Gordon and Bonnie Addington
and Evelyn Graves

You have always encouraged us
to live out our calling
Thank you
for that immeasurable gift.

Series Introduction

Our offices are on the fourth floor of the second tallest building in northwest Arkansas. We have an extraordinary view of the rolling hills of Fayetteville from our panoramic picture windows. Although our city is growing, it still has the feel of a small town. Almost everyone knows almost everyone.

From that vantage point we enjoy watching cycles of life unfold around us. Unlike some parts of the country, we benefit from the whole assortment of seasons. The snowy mantle of winter melts into the sweaty heat of summer, with all variations in between.

We also watch the daily routine of hundreds of businesses. At the start of a day we can see the lights of other businesses coming on, like eyes popping open after a good night's sleep. At the end of a day we witness those same lights going out. The next morning it begins all over again. Then again. Then again.

We talk to many men for whom that description sums up their work experience. People come and go, accounts open and close. Creditors get paid; customers get billed. We pick up; we deliver. We punch in; we punch out. The workday begins, then ends. We earn our money; we spend our money. The cycle is unrelenting and unending. Then the cycle quits, and we die.

Is that all there is? Is routine drudgery what a man should expect from his work life and career?

What is the difference in the behavior and experience of a Christian man in his work compared to that of a non-Christian man?

What does it mean to be a Christian who practices dentistry? Does it mean that I have Bible verses on my business card? Do I share Christ with patients while they are under anesthesia? Or perhaps I ought to treat only Christian patients. If someone doesn't pay me, should I send their bill into collections, or should I forgive the debt and maybe pay for it myself? Should I work longer hours to display an incredible work ethic? Or maybe I need to work shorter hours so that I can spend more time with my family or serve on a church or community committee. Do I pay my employees more than the national average? Or do I pay them less so they can learn to live by faith?

What does it mean to be a Christian plumber? Do I cut my rates for Christian customers? Should I work on Sunday, or do I fail to respond to a crisis that comes on the Sabbath? Perhaps I need to hand out gospel tracts to other subcontractors on the job. Should I release one of my crew if he's incompetent? Or are Christians bound to keep every employee on the payroll for life? What does the Bible say about work?

A number of years ago we came across a verse in the New Testament book of Acts that serves as God's final epitaph for King David:

When David had served God's purpose in his own generation, he fell asleep. (Acts 13:36)

Those words complete a description of David found way back in the Old Testament book of Psalms:

He chose David his servant and took him from the sheep pens; from tending the sheep he brought him to be the shepherd of his people Jacob, of Israel his inheritance. And David shepherded them with integrity of heart; with skillful hands he led them. (Psalm 78:70-72)

David was a shepherd, a musician, a soldier, and a king. He had a very busy, full, and successful career. We would like to use those verses about David as the basis for exploring the making of a godly man in and through his work world. This short series will consist of four parts:

....David... *served God's purpose...*: A Case for Calling

He chose *David his servant...*: A Case for Serving

....David shepherded them

with *integrity of heart*: A Case for Character

....with *skillful hands* he led them: A Case for Skill

So, we are back to one of our questions from above. Is work basically an unending and unfulfilling cycle of activity? Answer: it depends. On what? On whether or not I know God.

According to King Solomon, one of the wisest and wealthiest men of all time:

A man can do nothing better than to eat and drink and find satisfaction in his work. This too, I see, is from the hand of God.... *To the man who pleases him, God gives wisdom, knowledge and happiness, but to the sinner he gives the task of gathering and storing up wealth to hand*

it over to the one who pleases God. (Ecclesiastes 2:24-26; italics added)

Without God in my life, I might be driven, full of ambition, and very successful. I might even make it to the pinnacle of my profession. But I will not enjoy my work over time. It will not bring me fulfillment. I will be on a treadmill.

These books address a Christian man in the workplace. The definition and clarity that the Bible brings to a man and his work world are reserved for those who enjoy a personal relationship with Jesus. If you don't know Him, we strongly urge you to invite Him into your life. Then join us in exploring the topic of work in the incredibly rich, amazingly untapped pages of Scripture.

> May the favor of the Lord our God rest upon us;
> establish the work of our hands for us—
> yes, establish the work of our hands. (Psalm 90:17)

A word about our writing style. As coauthors, we speak in the first person when telling a story that relates to one of us as individuals. But we do not identify who belongs to which story. To help unravel that mystery, the following are some personal characteristics that will help sort us out.

Steve is an avid fisherman who baited hooks as a young boy on the Mississippi Gulf Coast. His appetite for learning and his energy for making friends have trademarked his twenty-three years of ministry and business.

Tom grew up in Hong Kong as the son of a medical missionary. He spent a number of years driving eighteen-wheelers, and he has taught at three universities.

We live in Fayetteville, Arkansas, love Scripture, and work together as business partners. Our companies and colleagues do work in organizational consulting and publishing. We have a passion to understand biblical principles that apply to work.

Book Introduction

Calling happens.

All Christian men are called. Individually. In regards to their work. I have been created by God to do something God wants me to do. When I know my calling and live it out, I am actually and literally part of fulfilling God's purpose.

To realize that is unbelievably wonderful. What could possibly be more fulfilling? My question is not, "Am I called?" Instead, my quest through life is, "What is my calling?"

This book helps define what calling is, and helps identify how I know my calling. What we learn might surprise us. But then, God is pretty good at doing that.

He has called me.

Definition of Calling

God's personal invitation for me
to work on his agenda,
using the talents I've been given
in ways that are eternally significant.

"When David had served God's purpose in his own generation, he fell asleep" (Acts 13:36).

CONTENTS

CHAPTER ONE

What Calling Is

I love to fish. Every year I go on a fishing expedition with three of my friends. I always look forward to it. I always come back the better for it. I love to fish.

Three of those annual trips have been on the Buffalo River in the Ozark National Forest, right here in Arkansas. The last twenty-five miles of the Buffalo, just before it dumps into the White River, is a remote wilderness area with no road access. The water is pristine clear; the cliffs are awesome and incredible; there is wildlife of every kind everywhere. It is peaceful and serene; you almost never see any other people.

It takes us four days of floating and camping to fish all the way to the White River. You haven't really lived until you have done a little top-water smallmouth-bass fishing on the last twenty-five miles of the Buffalo.

But I will never forget the beginning of the first day the first time we went. As usual, we were equipment heavy. We loaded all our food, camping apparatus, and fishing gear into the flat-bottomed eighteen-foot riverboats. We waved good-bye to the toothless stranger who had promised to deliver our cars to us at the end of the trip. We shoved off. We were on our way.

Less than four hundred yards into the twenty-five-mile trip is a sharp bend to the right. As we approached the turn we heard a noise that sounded distinctly like a waterfall. Or per-haps, waterfalls. Then our eyes confirmed what our ears had heard. Directly ahead of us was a steep drop. I couldn't believe it. We had been in the water less than five minutes, our cars were gone, and no one even expected to see us for four days.

We were not happy. There was some grumbling and mur-muring in the ranks along the line of: "I thought this was sup-posed to be the Buffalo, not Niagara." Then we huddled up and did all we knew to do. We got in the water and wrestled the boats, one by one, around the drop-off and through the rapids. Getting to four wonderful days of fishing meant that we had to navigate some rough water at the very beginning of the trip.

In the same way, getting to a meaningful career means that I first have to understand my calling. It is the initial key to figuring out my life at work.

As long as I have doubts about my calling, I will wonder if I am doing what I am supposed to be doing. Conversations with my wife will begin with words like: "I don't know, there just is something missing at work" or "I keep wondering if I should look into some other job possibilities" or "I wonder what else there is out there that might fit me better" or "I can't wait to retire so that I can..." or "I wish I could be more content with my work situation." If I don't know my calling, my work life will lack satisfaction.

But even more important, if I don't live out my calling, I compromise my ability to contribute to God's larger purpose with my work life and career. When the apostle Paul says, "David...served God's purpose in his own generation" (Acts 13:36), it is clear that God had a well-defined purpose for David's life work. In Scripture, "purpose" and "calling" are linked.

What is calling? What does it mean to be called in my work life? The answers to those questions are hidden in three principles from Scripture:

1. As a godly man I am called to serve God's purpose.

2. I have a calling that is work-specific.

3. God has given me a unique gift mix for my work.

It's to serve God's purpose.

My dad is a called man. He lives as meaningful a life as anyone I know. Well into retirement, he works tirelessly on a project that he believes God wants him to finish. But this current undertaking is only the latest evidence of God's obvious call on his seventy-plus-year life.

As a young man who had just completed seminary, he and Mom were convinced that they belonged in missions. When the mission organization told him that they really needed doctors, he promptly enrolled in medical school.

He arrived in Hong Kong in 1960 as a young physician to open an outpatient clinic. But because of the unmanageable influx of refugees from China, the Hong Kong Medical Department urged him to build an inpatient hospital. Evangel Hospital was dedicated in 1965 and to this day provides excellent medical care regardless of a patient's ability to pay.

Dad completed a residency in general surgery when it became clear that a surgeon was needed at the hospital, and none was available.

Later in his career when he returned to the United States, he practiced as a surgeon with the same sense of calling. He was at various times chief of surgery and chief of staff at a large hospital in St. Paul.

The list could go on. It would only emphasize and confirm what people who know my dad say about him: he is a man deeply aware of his calling.

Calling is God's personal invitation for me to work on *His* agenda, using the talents I've been given in ways that are eternally significant. To be called means I know that what I am doing is what God wants me to do. Furthermore, when I live within God's calling, not only does my work give me a sense of meaning, but it also fits into God's larger purpose.

Scripture clearly links my calling with God's purpose: "We know that in all things God works for the good of those who love him, who have been called according to his purpose" (Romans 8:28). My individual calling is absolutely connected with His purpose. I am being called in order to fit into His purpose.

My work is not some arbitrary and random choice that makes no difference. Its primary objective is not to put food on the table and provide a comfortable retirement. My individual, personal, just-me work calling is part of God's larger agenda in history. I actually have a part in God's plan.

The biblical concept of calling is confusing if we don't understand the difference and connection between calling, purpose, and meaning. They are not the same thing, but they are closely connected.

PURPOSE

Purpose in Scripture is synonymous with God's sovereign design, His overarching view of history, what He is accomplishing. Very few men in the Bible knew exactly what His purpose was during their lifetime. Some of the prophets did, at least to some extent. We know God's purpose only if He chooses to reveal it to us.

We are to serve God's purpose, whatever it is, even though we do not necessarily know all the details. Here is what we do know:

1. God operates off of a master plan, even though He doesn't always tell us what it is.
2. God specifically fits each of us as Christians into the larger workings of His overall plan.
3. We serve His purpose through faith by knowing His calling on our lives.

We meet men who think their purpose will be fulfilled whenever they make it to the next rung on the ladder or whenever they become their own boss and launch their own company. They are being pulled to do something bigger, but that search for purpose is always outside their grasp.

As Christian men, we know our work has purpose because we are serving a God whose purpose is bigger than us. To look up into the night sky at the end of the day and know that our work and life are part of His bigger plan supplies an inner joy and satisfaction that can come from nothing else.

CALLING

If purpose is something I have to serve, calling is something I need to know. Calling is what I do individually to fit into God's purpose. Some verses about calling refer to God's call on my life to become His child, as well as His call on my life regarding work or vocation. Other Scripture passages talk specifically about God's calling concerning work. Because I am "called according to His purpose," it is imperative that I discover exactly what my calling is. According to Ephesians: "In him we were also chosen [or called], having been predestined according to the plan of him who works out everything in conformity with the purpose of his will" (Ephesians 1:11).

God calls us to serve in a way that is consistent with how He has designed us. Finding my calling is about learning how God has designed me to serve Him.

MEANING

God's purpose is something I serve. My calling is something I know. Meaning is something I am to enjoy. If I am accurately living out my calling, I will experience the incredible sense of meaning from my work that only God can provide.

King Solomon was one of the wisest and wealthiest men of all time. He was a very successful king with an innate sense of how to do a financial deal. But his special gift from God was in the realm of wisdom. He had plenty of it.

Solomon wrote Ecclesiastes near the end of his life. He devotes portions of the Old Testament book to different topics, like wisdom, pleasure, and knowledge. But one entire part is devoted to work. In that section Solomon hammers at the theme that a godly man will find meaning, satisfaction, and fulfillment in his work:

A man can do nothing better than to eat and drink and find satisfaction in his work. This too, I see, is from the hand of God, for without him, who can eat or find enjoyment? (2:24-25)

I know that there is nothing better for men than to be happy and do good while they live. That every man may eat and drink, and find satisfaction in all his toil—this is the gift of God. (3:12-13)

So I saw that there is nothing better for a man than to enjoy his work, because that is his lot. (3:22)

Then I realized that it is good and proper for a man to eat and drink, and to find satisfaction in his toilsome

labor under the sun during the few days of life God has
given him—for this is his lot. (5:18)

Who receives the gift of work-related meaning? Everyone?
Negative. Only those who are godly:

To the man who pleases him, God gives wisdom,
knowledge and happiness, but to the sinner he gives
the task of gathering and storing up wealth to hand it
over to the one who pleases God. (2:26)

A non-Christian in the work world does not have nearly
the sense of meaning in his career that a Christian experiences.
He does the work. But he does not receive the same enjoyment,
the same meaning, the same satisfaction available to a
Christian. Only a Christian can serve God's purpose, can know
God's calling, and can experience God's gift of meaning.

We are to serve purpose. We are to know calling. We are to
enjoy meaning.

It's work-specific.

Jeremiah was one of God's prophets who played a crucial
role in Old Testament Jewish history. The record of his calling

gives us a unique window into what God has in mind for us regarding our work.

God set Jeremiah apart before he was even born, with a specific work purpose in mind: "Before you were born I set you apart," God said. Why? Because, "I appointed you as a prophet to the nations" (Jeremiah 1:5).

In this passage, Jeremiah's life had purpose because his work had purpose.

All men are called to work. Work is not a curse. Genesis documents God's work agenda for Adam before the Fall: "The Lord God took the man and put him in the Garden of Eden to work it and take care of it" (2:15).

In the next chapter we see God's work agenda after the Fall: "So the Lord God banished him from the Garden of Eden to work the ground from which he had been taken" (3:23).

Work is not a curse. But the curse—that came as a result of the Fall—made work much harder:

Cursed is the ground because of you; *through painful toil you will eat of it all the days of your life. It will pro-duce thorns and thistles for you, and you will eat the plants of the field. By the sweat of your brow you will eat your food until you return to the ground,* since from it you were taken; for dust you are and to dust you will return. (Genesis 3:17-19; italics added)

The curse added a real sense of "sweat" and "making a living is going to be hard," but it did not remove the dignity and meaning from work. Nowhere in Scripture is work to be avoided. Nowhere in Scripture is work described as an unfortunate necessity that we must do only so that we can do "real fun stuff" like vacations, weekends, and retirements. Work is not a punishment or an afterthought. Quite the opposite, my calling from Jesus is work-specific. That all means that we should bring a tremendous energy and enthusiasm with us to work.

I drove tractor-trailer rigs for several years. It was always interesting to sit in the driver's lounge and listen to other drivers talk while our trucks were being loaded. Regardless of where I was in the country, the discussion revolved around the following four topics (the language has been sanitized):

1. My dispatcher is incompetent; he is out to get me and I am out to get him.
2. My job does not pay enough.

3. My company always tries to cheat me out of what they owe me.

4. No state trooper ever cuts me enough slack.

It took only five words to render everyone speechless, for a dead silence to descend on stunned men holding coffee cups. The words? "I like what I do." Whenever I uttered those words everyone sort of looked at the floor, cleared their throats, then announced that they needed to go check on when their trucks would be loaded. Conversation, as they knew it, was over.

If we are called, and if we are doing what we are called to do, we should be able to say that with conviction and without blushing. We ought to work hard and enjoy doing it. We should not have to apologize that we like to work and that we look forward to getting up in the morning and getting to the job. Nor should we have to buy into the notion that Mondays are terrible, compared with Fridays that are wonderful.

But we also need to be careful. Work is not the sum total of our life, nor was it ever meant to be. We must never hide behind our calling as an excuse for our work to own us in inappropriate ways. In our personal experience, and also from our conversations with hundreds of men over the years, there are at least three common traps that we need to run from:

1. *Allowing work to drive me*

There is a big difference between a driven man and a called man. Among other things, a driven man often allows the demands of the job to set the agenda for his life. "I am busy because I can't help it, because the job demands it," so the thinking goes. As work heats up, as the company grows, as the promotions come, as the number of customers increase, as the phone rings more often, I have no choice but to run faster, devote more hours, stay up later, get up earlier, travel more often.

As a called man, I will work very hard. But it is Jesus who is calling me, not my job. Unless we understand that distinction, the job that Jesus calls us to can actually end up calling us away from Jesus.

Drivenness emanates from internal restlessness, a never-satisfied striving, pride, and ego. Calling comes from knowing what I am supposed to do to fit into God's overarching purpose. It is Jesus who calls me, and in doing so He brings satisfaction, rest, a sense of togetherness, completeness, and whole-ness. The Jesus who calls us also calls out to us:

> Come to me, all you who are weary and burdened, and
> I will give you rest. Take my yoke upon you and learn
> from me, for I am gentle and humble in heart, and you
> will find rest for your souls. For my yoke is easy and
> my burden is light. (Matthew 11:28-30)

2. *Asking work to supply my identity*

When I became a Christian my name was recorded in the Lamb's Book of Life. Nowhere does Scripture indicate that my occupation will be recorded alongside my name. My identity comes from Christ.

How Paul saw himself, before he met Jesus, was directly tied to what he did as a Pharisee. His work supplied his iden-tity. One gets the impression that the list was well rehearsed:

> Circumcised on the eighth day, of the people of Israel,
> of the tribe of Benjamin, a Hebrew of Hebrews; in
> regard to the law, a Pharisee; as for zeal, persecuting the
> church; as for legalistic righteousness, faultless.
> (Philippians 3:5-6)

But after he became a Christian, he switched his identity from his work to his Lord: "But whatever was to my profit I now consider loss for the sake of Christ. I want to know Christ" (Philippians 3:7, 10).

3.   *Using work to ignore my family*

A number of years ago I was with the founder of a major retailer as he addressed a group. In a moment of candor, the man related that members of his family were unhappy with all the time he was spending growing the company. He kept promising his wife, "Just one more store." Finally, his wife quit asking and he stopped promising, because both of them knew he was going to continue regardless.

We no longer have any excuse for not giving our families a balanced portion of our time and attention. Promise Keepers has addressed more men on that topic than any other topic. Authors like Gary Smalley, Wellington Boone, John Trent, James Dobson, Dennis Rainey, and Steve Farrar give us tremendous help in knowing how to be a good husband and father.

A calling to work does not take away from our privileges, obligations, joys, and pleasures of home life. If, over time, our work ends up stealing from the family, we have misunderstood how calling at work intersects with life at home.

It fits my unique gift mix

The men in our consulting company could not be more different in how we approach our work. We do similar tasks. We service the same clients. We share the same values. We use the same technology. But we could not be more different.

Some of us come at our work like engineers. Engineers operate best when a process is in place or can be designed. We love systems. We say things like " A good process turns out a good product." We are very organized. Our thinking is linear. We love to put information into specific categories. Knowing and following procedure are important. In our way of thinking, the best work is done behind the scenes, in preparation for rolling it out in public.

Others of us are in our best element as facilitators in a fast-moving meeting full of complex problems and difficult issues. We revel in free flow of information and ideas. Put us in a pressure situation where we have to think on our feet and figure things out on the spot, and we will shine. In our way of thinking, the best work is done in public. Behind-the-scenes preparation is OK, but it may not prove to be that relevant.

Then we have men who are a distinctive blend of a number of approaches. There is unbelievable richness in working with men with diverse makeup. We have different approaches to the same issues. Our perspectives are diverse and complement each other. The fact that we have different makeup is a good thing.

God gives us a unique gift mix for our work. We are all made differently. Listen to David reflect on the wonder of how God knows and uniquely makes up an individual:

> O Lord, you have searched me
>> and you know me.
> You know when I set and when I rise;
>> you perceive my thoughts from afar.
> You discern my going out and my lying down;
>> you are familiar with all my ways....
> For you created my inmost being;
>> you knit me together in my mother's womb.
> I praise you because I am fearfully
>> and wonderfully made;

your works are wonderful,
I know that full well.
My frame was not hidden from you
    when I was made in the secret place.
When I was woven together in the depths of the earth,
    your eyes saw my unformed body.
All the days ordained for me
    were written in your book
    before one of them came to be. (Psalm 139)

My makeup and gift mix are an extremely significant indicator of my calling. I was designed from the very beginning by God to accomplish His purpose. Based on David's psalm, would it make any sense for God to form and equip me with such precise intention, and then call me to do something that does not fit who I am? Just like our fingerprints uniquely identify us, God receives the greatest glory when our gifts find their full expression. He is not glorified when we try to be someone we were never intended to be or created to be. We might articulate that rich truth in the following way:

If God created me to serve His purpose, and if God formed and "wired" me with awesomely precise intention, then my calling should be closely aligned with my makeup.

We might have questions that revolve around the exact nature of our calling. But we should never wonder if God has made us up internally to accomplish our calling. I have been created with the exact gift mix to do what God wants me to do.

CHAPTER TWO

Four Categories for How Calling Happens

How does God call me? We researched the answer to that question by going directly to the pages of Scripture. In the Old and New Testaments there are scores of examples of men called by God into specific work situations. God's methods of calling fit into four categories:

Category 1: God calls me directly by name.

Category 2: God places a desire on my heart.

Category 3: God arranges my path.

Category 4: God prepares an attractive option.

Category 1: God calls me directly by name.

ABRAHAM

Genesis 12 begins rather abruptly: "The Lord had said to Abram, 'Leave your country, your people and your father's household and go to the land I will show you'" (Genesis 12:1).

OK! What can Abram (his name until God changed it to Abraham) say? God's call on his life was so clear, so precise, so unambiguous that there really was only one possible response.

> So Abram left, as the Lord had told him.... Abram was seventy-five years old when he set out from Haran. He took his wife Sarai, his nephew Lot, all the possessions they had accumulated and the people they had acquired in Haran, and they set out for the land of Canaan, and they arrived there. (Genesis 12:4-5)

Who else experienced God's call in a similar way?

MOSES

Moses was called by name:

> Now Moses was tending the flock of Jethro his father-in-law... and he led the flock to the far side of the

desert and came to Horeb, the mountain of God. There the angel of the Lord appeared to him in flames of fire from within a bush. Moses saw that though the bush was on fire it did not burn up. So Moses thought, "I will go over and see this strange sight—why the bush does not burn up."

When the Lord saw that he had gone over to look, God called to him from within the bush, "Moses, Moses!"

And Moses said, "Here I am."

.... The Lord said, "... So now, go. I am sending you to Pharaoh to bring my people the Israelites out of Egypt." (Exodus 3:1-10)

Moses did not appreciate God's call very much, "O Lord, please send someone else to do it," but he was not left in much doubt as to what God's call was.

PAUL

Paul's call was also very dramatic. He was on his way to Damascus to persecute and imprison any Christians he found there, when Jesus confronted Paul with a light bright enough to blind him. Simultaneous with the light Paul heard the words:

> "Saul, Saul, why do you persecute me?"
> "Who are you, Lord?" Saul asked.
> "I am Jesus, whom you are persecuting," he replied. "Now get up and go into the city, and you will be told what you must do." (Acts 9:4-6)

Over the next few days God used a man by the name of Ananias to communicate His specific calling to Paul. The encounter changed Paul's life. Not only did he end up with a new relationship with the God of the universe, he also had a new calling and career.

God's call to Abraham, to Moses, and to Paul could not have been more direct. God addressed them directly by name and told them what their work was going to look like. In the same category are Old Testament men like Joshua, Aaron, Ezekiel, Samson, and Elijah. The New Testament list includes Matthew, Peter, James, and John the Baptist.

Sometimes God addresses me directly and calls me by name.

Category 2: God places a desire on my heart.

NEHEMIAH

Nehemiah was a troubled man. Close to the apex of power in Babylon, he had access to information. And what he heard one day caused him to sit down and weep. The walls around Jerusalem were lying in rubble, and the gates had been burned to the ground.

Nehemiah's response was dramatic: "When I heard these things, I sat down and wept. For some days I mourned and fasted and prayed before the God of heaven" (Nehemiah 1:4). He was devastated. The walls were down around the "city on a hill" that symbolized God's chosen nation. How could the Jews return from exile in Babylon to a city that lay vulnerable, unprotected, and in disgrace?

Why did the news about Jerusalem affect Nehemiah with such force? Was he so ignorant about suffering and injustice in the world that a bad report left him stunned? Of course not. He was the cupbearer to King Artaxerxes of Babylon, which was the dominant empire of the day. In today's world, Nehemiah's position would be similar to the White House chief of staff. Nehemiah heard bad news, shocking information, extremely unsettling data every hour of every working day. It goes with the territory of such a position.

But this news was different. It affected him uniquely because God wanted it to. God had it in His plan to use Nehemiah to lead the effort to rebuild the wall. The Babylonian exile was ending, and God's people were returning to the Promised Land. Nehemiah was a crucial component of God's plan to bring His people home. The burden placed on Nehemiah's heart was God's unavoidable call to a very specific task.

ISAIAH

Nehemiah heard terrible news, but Isaiah had a wonderful vision. He saw the Lord seated on a throne in the highest heaven. Above the throne were magnificent angels, each with six wings. As the angels flew they sang perpetually, "Holy, holy, holy is the Lord Almighty; the whole earth is full of his glory" (Isaiah 6:3).

There was smoke, and everything shook. Isaiah was so taken with the purity of God that his own unrighteousness overwhelmed him. He was a broken man: "'Woe to me!'" I cried. 'I am ruined! For I am a man of unclean lips, and I live among a people of unclean lips, and my eyes have seen the King, the Lord Almighty'" (Isaiah 6:5).

Then something remarkable happened. One of the angels took a live coal, touched Isaiah's mouth, and declared Isaiah's guilt gone and his sin atoned for. In an interchange that followed, God asked who would represent him, and Isaiah volunteered: "'Here am I. Send me!'" (Isaiah 6:8).

So launched the career of one of the major prophets of the Old Testament era. God called Isaiah to be His spokesman to the nation of Israel during a very turbulent time.

Sometimes I feel a responsibility to accomplish a task and meet a need (or, God places a burden on my heart).

Category 3: God arranges my path.

DANIEL

The British Museum in London has a stone panel from the palace of King Nebuchadnezzar, which depicts captives being led in chains from Jerusalem to Babylon. I have stood in front of that amazing pictorial many times, and in every instance I have thought about Daniel. Daniel was called to his career in disgrace. He was one of the captives taken from his home in the Promised Land to the capital of a powerful and pagan empire.

Daniel was called to serve and rose to be a top administrator during almost the entire captivity of the Israelites in Babylon. He did so with utmost integrity, and often at risk to his own life. In one of the most spectacular conversions of all time, Nebuchadnezzar, who was one of the cruelest rulers of his day, became a follower of God though Daniel's influence: "Now I, Nebuchadnezzar, praise and exalt and glorify the King of heaven, because everything he does is right and all his ways are just. And those who walk in pride he is able to humble" (Daniel 4:37).

Daniel served four kings in three empires. He was so valuable that even when the empire changed hands, from the Babylonians to the Medes to the Persians, Daniel stayed in place. He was very good at what he did. He was called to his career. As a captive, he had no choice.

JOSIAH

When Josiah came out of the womb, his life career had already been decided; he just didn't know it yet. But he found out quickly. He was eight years old when he became king of

Judah, and he ruled in Jerusalem for thirty-one years (2 Kings 22).

Josiah was a direct descendant of David, the great king of Israel. During David's reign God promised him that his house, or family, would rule forever. So as with the House of Windsor in Great Britain, whose clearly established line of succession determines who rules next, Josiah was born into royal obligation.

Josiah was called to be king. His calling and career did not involve any choice on his part. There were no list of options from what to choose. His calling was decided for him.

Sometimes a job simply shows up at my door (or, God arranges my career track without my input).

Category 4: God prepares an attractive option.

ELISHA

Elisha's calling was almost cryptic, but then I guess that is what you would expect if you were recruited by a prophet. Elisha was working on the farm. More specifically, he was plowing with twelve yoke of oxen. All of the sudden Elijah the prophet came up to him and threw his cloak around him.

Elisha then left his oxen and ran after Elijah. "Let me kiss my father and mother good-by," he said, "and then I will come with you." "Go back," Elijah replied. "What have I done to you?" So Elisha left him and went back. He took his yoke of oxen and slaughtered them. He burned the plowing equipment to cook the meat and gave it to the people, and they ate. Then he set out to follow Elijah and became his attendant. (1 Kings 19:20-21)

Elisha had an extraordinary career. He was mentored by Elijah, until Elijah was suddenly taken up to heaven in a whirlwind of chariots and horses of fire. Then Elisha was on his own. Somehow he felt called to choose a relationship and a career with Elijah. Which was exactly what God had created him to do.

STEPHEN

We remember Stephen primarily because he was stoned to death for his faith. He was the first Christian martyr, following Christ's ascension into heaven. But he first comes to our attention in Acts 6.

The young church in Jerusalem was straining under the weight of its exponential growth. The apostles, who were called to lead the church, found themselves consumed with a myriad of operational details. They decided that a different organizational structure was needed.

> So the Twelve gathered all the disciples together and said, "It would not be right for us to neglect the ministry of the word of God in order to wait on tables [the operational problem of the moment]. Brothers, choose seven men from among you who are known to be full of the Spirit and wisdom. We will turn this responsibility over to them and will give our attention to prayer and the ministry of the word." (Acts 6:2-4)

Stephen was one of those chosen. It might have looked to be a simple case of being in the right place at the right time. He just happened to be available. But Stephen's calling was far more than simple coincidence. God, in his sovereignty, had prepared Stephen and placed him exactly where he could be "chosen." What looked like a serendipitous employment opportunity was really God's way of calling a man.

Sometimes I respond to an employment opportunity (or, I am led to "choose" a work option that God prepared and made attractive).

God uses different ways to call me regarding my work. Apart from a direct word from God, the work I am called to often looks and feels like the coincidental intersection between a job opportunity, my makeup, and leading from the Holy Spirit. The next chapter paints a picture of three current-day examples of what calling looks like.

CHAPTER THREE

What Calling Looks Like

C alling of men does not only happen in the pages of
Scripture. As is clear from what we have learned in
this book, all of us are called.

Larry Wheeler (not his real name), Milton Lentz, and Rich
Brown are all friends of ours. They are "called" men, but to different careers. Larry is a top executive in a Fortune 50 company. Milton owns his own construction company. Rich is a
physician and surgeon. What follows is a description of each of
their callings.

The executive: Larry Wheeler

Larry Wheeler heard a calling when he graduated from college, but it wasn't from the Lord.

As one of the top graduates from Ohio University in 1970,
Larry was getting calls from all quarters—including Harvard

Business School. The one he decided to answer, though, was from a large multinational corporation.

Larry had seen enough of the classroom. He was ready for the boardroom. He was ready to make his move onto the corporate fast track, where he just knew he would lap the field.

And he did, too. But in rising to a position as a vice president of a Fortune 50 company, Larry discovered that another plan, one larger and much more dynamic than his own, also was in the works. And as he rose up each rung of the corporate ladder, he not only achieved secular success but placed himself in a position for spiritual success as well.

Larry was living in the town of his company's corporate offices when he discovered Christ. But it wasn't until he moved to another location and launched an innovative customer business development division that he gained a real sense of his calling and how it fit into his professional life.

In helping engineer a partnership relationship with his company's largest customer, Larry began to explore the idea of linking business principles with biblical wisdom. Every time a decision had to be made in this highly stressful, ultracompetitive secular business setting, he turned to the Bible for practical solutions. And every time he turned to look for answers, God provided them.

Despite resistance from top executives at both companies, God continued to affirm and reaffirm Larry's approach with answers to problems and positive bottom-line results that silenced the critics.

The model Larry helped develop now is used worldwide by his company, even though many of those who are using it are unaware that the ideas behind it came not from a business book but from the greatest best-seller of all time—the Bible.

Larry is a mentor and a leader to other men all over the world, not just for his extraordinary talents as an executive, but also for his steady display of godly character.

But Larry has been able to model on more than just a personal level. While that is an important part of his calling in the workplace, it is only one part. Another is the actual model he helped create for his company—a model founded and constructed with biblical principles and yet a model that significantly outperforms systems designed by man.

The examples of his life and the business system he helped create serve as testimonies for numerous men and women at numerous different levels within the secular world. They allow others to see how the power and wisdom of God can work outside of what traditionally are considered "religious" settings.

The builder: Milton Lentz

The foundations for the eight thousand-square-foot house are dug into a hilltop that overlooks other hilltops and valleys and all of the other wonders of this particular edge of the Ozark Mountains.

When it is completed, the owner will have a majestic view, one befitting his status as a well-to-do member of an area filled with well-to-do members. He will be able to pull his expensive car through his expensive gate and drive up his expensive drive to an expensive house filled with expensive furnishings.

But he will rest easily in the knowledge that this project was a bargain. For one thing, he knows the man building it for him would never cheat him by padding his bills or cutting corners. It just wouldn't happen. And when he opens his eyes and his heart, he finds an even-more-valuable fringe benefit from the construction firm he hired—the quiet example of the man who owns it.

Milton Lentz wasn't just called to work in the construction business, he was born into it.

When he was three years old and his father headed off to a construction site, Milton went right along with him, just as his father had done at the hands of Milton's grandfather.

If his father had been a mechanic, Milton might well be a mechanic today. But his father worked in construction. And for most of his forty-two years on this earth, so has Milton.

However, Milton learned early on that he wasn't being forced into a vocation simply to maintain the family tradition. He discovered he had real talents that merely were being developed by his environment. Milton can hammer a two-inch nail into a four-inch-wide board directly above his head faster than most men can pull that same nail from the pouch in their work belt.

Milton tested the waters once. As a young adult he went to work at a carpet store. It didn't take long for Milton to realize he wasn't a salesman. For one thing, he was too color-blind to tell customers honestly if this carpet matched that wallpaper. For another, he simply wasn't cut out to push products on a daily basis.

Luckily, Milton's house burned. It didn't seem so lucky at the time, of course. But that misfortune provided an insurance check that allowed Milton to escape what fast was becoming a suffocating job and the debt that was coming with it.

So Milton returned to a more natural calling, one that God had confirmed to him many times before and would confirm to him many times after.

Milton sees that confirmation in the projects he voluntarily built at several locations across the country for the Torchbearers of the Capernwray Missionary Fellowship which operates Bible schools and summer camps.

He sees that confirmation in each new client, especially those who show up unexpectedly when they are needed the most. He couldn't make a living selling carpet, he will point out, but God continues to provide homes and offices for him to build.

And he sees that confirmation in people like the man who wants the big house up on the hill. Milton never brings up God when he is working on that job. He never forces his testimony on the man who is paying the bills. But the man simply can't resist asking, because he can't help seeing God work through the life of his contractor.

The surgeon: Rich Brown

It wasn't until Rich Brown gave up on his dream to become an eye surgeon that God helped it come true.

After four years of college and four years of medical school, Rich was ready to begin his residency in ophthalmology (if you can spell it, he says, you're board certified). He was fascinated by the eye and vividly recalled the two surgeries he needed as a child to straighten the muscles surrounding his eyes. This, it seemed, was his calling.

Rich always had a general sense of what God wanted him to do with his professional life. But the older he has become, the more specific that call has become.

He grew up in a Christian home. The fact that God had a plan for him was taught at an early age, and he never really considered that he might do something that wasn't in line with God's purpose.

By the time he was ready to graduate from elementary school, Rich already felt a calling for service. And by dreaming and praying about what that meant, he soon was led into medicine. His family had a history of attending college, but he would be the first doctor.

He spent a year at West Point learning that he did not want to become a military doctor. But he still knew he wanted to practice medicine. It wasn't until he was in medical school that he began to think about the eye surgeries he had undergone as a child. While walking home from class each day, he began to think about a career in vision.

But when it came time to find a residency, Rich faced one rather large problem: He had nowhere to go.

Like all would-be doctors, Rich had submitted his list of preferred residency choices. The residency programs submitted their lists of preferred doctors. When the two lists came together, there was no match for Rich in ophthalmology.

Naturally, he was devastated—so devastated, in fact, that he ended up in a mental hospital. Not as a patient, although he admits that maybe he should have been. Rich was working part-time as a night admissions officer at a mental-health facility in Little Rock. The workload was light, so Rich turned his attention to prayer. Despite his desire to become an eye surgeon, he gave his career over to God. He would do, he said, whatever God instructed, even if it meant a residency in his least favorite of fields—ob-gyn.

Suddenly, a peace came over Rich Brown. For the first time since he learned the news about his residency, he was able to rest.

The next morning, two hours into a shift at Arkansas Children's Hospital, Rich got a call from his father. It seems a doctor at the University of Missouri-Kansas City had been unable to reach Rich through other channels, and he needed to talk to the young physician. UMKC had an unexpected opening the doctor thought Rich could fill—a residency in ophthalmology.

Rich, now thirty-nine with ten years of experience as an ophthalmologist, has seen that calling confirmed in many ways. He has seen it in the people he works with—patients, doctors, and staff. He has seen it in the amount of time being in his profession gives him to devote to other ministries. And he saw it three years ago when he was having a crisis in confidence while trying to adjust to new surgical techniques. His colleagues rallied to support him and reaffirmed his natural talent for surgery.

But his most recent confirmation that he is serving where God wants him came when he and his family were selected for a work-mission trip in Gilgit, Pakistan, for the 1997 summer.

When Rich e-mailed the dates he would be available, he got a quick and enthusiastic reply. The dates corresponded with the dates when one of the two doctors at the clinic would be in London for a training course. He would be coming at the time the clinic needed him most—there to help man and serve God as an ophthalmologist, just as he had originally dreamed.

Conclusion

Calling is God's personal invitation for each Christian to work on His agenda, utilizing our created talents to do something that is eternally significant.

Finding and living out our calling are absolutely essential steps in the making of a godly man. If we know our calling, then we can serve God's purpose and enjoy meaning and satisfaction.

On our Buffalo River fishing trip a couple of years ago, we had to navigate around some very rough water before we could delight in the heaven-on-earth exhilaration that every true fisherman knows.

Calling is very much the same. The earlier in our work life that we discover our calling, the longer we will have to revel in our job fit and delight in our career niche.

Calling happens. Why? Because God loves us enough to create us with precision and use us for something eternally significant.

Thank you, Lord.

"When David had served God's purpose in his own generation, he fell asleep" (Acts 13:36).

Where Do I Go from Here?

1. *Come to God in brokenness, with an intense passion to understand His Word and hear His voice.*

   We will only know our calling if He tells us. He is the key to our calling. Finding our calling is a spiritual exercise in which I turn my face toward God in both Bible study and prayer, with specific intent to know His will regarding my vocation.

2. *Pray, think, and talk your way through chapter 2, "Four Categories for How Calling Happens."*

   As you look back on your pilgrimage through life and as you evaluate your present situation, what clues do you have to help explain your calling? What do people who know you well say about your calling when they look at you through the lens of the four categories?

3. *Distinguish between the kind of work you do and the actual job you have.*

If you are unhappy in your current situation, determine whether your dissatisfaction comes from the kind of work your job requires, or from your work environment, or from both. Our best reading of Scripture leaves us convinced that God calls us to do the kind of work we are suited for. However, He may call us to do the kind of work that we are suited for in an environment that is very imperfect. Figuring out what action to take depends on knowing the reasons for your unhappiness.

4. *Be patient.*

God makes His will clear to us in His time. We cannot rush what He is not doing quickly. View this as a process over time, not an event in time.

Notes for Personal Reflection

Chapter One

_____

_____

_____

_____

_____

_____

_____

_____

_____

_____

_____

_____

_____

_____

_____

Chapter Two

_____

_____

_____

_____

_____

_____

_____

_____

_____

_____

_____

_____

_____

_____

_____

_____

_____

Chapter Three

_____

_____

_____

_____

_____

_____

_____

_____

_____

_____

_____

_____

_____

_____

_____

_____

_____

If you liked this book and would like to know more about ™Life@Work Co.™ or Cornerstone please call us at 1-800-739-7863.

Other ways to reach us:

    Mail: Post Office Box 1928
                 Fayetteville, AR 72702

    Fax: (501) 443-4125

    E-mail: LifeWork@CornerstoneCo.com

A CASE FOR
Character

Also by ^{THE} Life@Work Co.™

A Case for Calling
A Case for Skill
A Case for Serving

A CASE FOR
Character

Discovering the Difference a Godly Man Makes in His Life at Work

DR. STEPHEN GRAVES & DR. THOMAS ADDINGTON

Cornerstone *Alliance*
FAYETTEVILLE, ARKANSAS 72702

Published by Cornerstone Alliance
Post Office Box 1928
Fayetteville, AR 72702

ISBN 1-890581-02-X

Cover design by Sean Womack of Cornerstone Alliance.

Printed in the United States of America

1 3 5 7 9 10 8 6 4 2

To our children

Katelyn, Julianne, Kile
Kim, Sally, Joel

Remember Proverbs 22:1.

Series Introduction

Our offices are on the fourth floor of the second tallest building in northwest Arkansas. We have an extraordinary view of the rolling hills of Fayetteville from our panoramic picture windows. Although our city is growing, it still has the feel of a small town. Almost everyone knows almost everyone.

From that vantage point we enjoy watching cycles of life unfold around us. Unlike some parts of the country, we benefit from the whole assortment of seasons. The snowy mantle of winter melts into the sweaty heat of summer, with all variations in between.

We also watch the daily routine of hundreds of businesses. At the start of a day we can see the lights of other businesses coming on, like eyes popping open after a good night's sleep. At the end of a day we witness those same lights going out. The next morning it begins all over again. Then again. Then again.

We talk to many men for whom that description sums up their work experience. People come and go; accounts open and close. Creditors get paid; customers get billed. We pick up; we deliver. We punch in; we punch out. The workday begins, then ends. We earn our money; we spend our money. The cycle is unrelenting and unending. Then the cycle quits, and we die.

Is that all there is? Is routine drudgery what a man should expect from his work life and career?

What is the difference in the behavior and experience of a Christian man in his work compared to that of a non-Christian man?

What does it mean to be a Christian who practices dentistry? Does it mean that I have Bible verses on my business card? Do I share Christ with patients while they are under anesthesia? Or perhaps I ought to treat only Christian patients. If someone doesn't pay me, should I send their bill into collections, or should I forgive the debt and maybe pay for it myself? Should I work longer hours to display an incredible work ethic? Or maybe I need to work shorter hours so that I can spend more time with my family or serve on a church or community committee. Do I pay my employees more than the national average? Or do I pay them less so they can learn to live by faith?

What does it mean to be a Christian plumber? Do I cut my rates for Christian customers? Should I work on Sunday, or do I fail to respond to a crisis that comes on the Sabbath? Perhaps I need to hand out gospel tracts to other subcontractors on the job. Should I release one of my crew if he's incompetent? Or are Christians bound to keep every employee on the payroll for life? What does the Bible say about work?

A number of years ago we came across a verse in the New Testament book of Acts that serves as God's final epitaph for King David:

> When David had served God's purpose in his own generation, he fell asleep. (Acts 13:36)

Those words complete a description of David found way back in the Old Testament book of Psalms:

> He chose David his servant and took him from the sheep pens; from tending the sheep he brought him to be the shepherd of his people Jacob, of Israel his inheritance. And David shepherded them with integrity of heart; with skillful hands he led them. (Psalm 78:70-72)

David was a shepherd, a musician, a soldier, and a king. He had a very busy, full, and successful career. We would like to use those verses about David as the basis for exploring the making of a godly man in and through his work world. This short series will consist of four parts:

....David... *served God's purpose...*: A Case for Calling
He chose *David his servant...*: A Case for Serving
....David shepherded them
   with *integrity of heart*: A Case for Character
....with *skillful hands* he led them: A Case for Skill

So, we are back to one of our questions from above. Is work basically an unending and unfulfilling cycle of activity? Answer: it depends. On what? On whether or not I know God.

According to King Solomon, one of the wisest and wealthiest men of all time:

A man can do nothing better than to eat and drink and find satisfaction in his work. This too, I see, is from the hand of God.... *To the man who pleases him, God gives wisdom, knowledge and happiness, but to the sinner he gives the task of gathering and storing up wealth to hand*

it over to the one who pleases God. (Ecclesiastes 2:24-26; italics added)

Without God in my life, I might be driven, full of ambition, and very successful. I might even make it to the pinnacle of my profession. But I will not enjoy my work over time. It will not bring me fulfillment. I will be on a treadmill.

These books address a Christian man in the workplace. The definition and clarity that the Bible brings to a man and his work world are reserved for those who enjoy a personal relationship with Jesus. If you don't know Him, we strongly urge you to invite Him into your life. Then join us in exploring the topic of work in the incredibly rich, amazingly untapped pages of Scripture.

May the favor of the Lord our God rest upon us;
establish the work of our hands for us—
yes, establish the work of our hands. (Psalm 90:17)

A word about our writing style. As coauthors, we speak in the first person when telling a story that relates to one of us as individuals. But we do not identify who belongs to which story. To help unravel that mystery, the following are some personal characteristics that will help sort us out.

Steve is an avid fisherman who baited hooks as a young boy on the Mississippi Gulf Coast. His appetite for learning and his energy for making friends have trademarked his twenty-three years of ministry and business.

Tom grew up in Hong Kong as the son of a medical missionary. He spent a number of years driving eighteen-wheelers, and he has taught at three universities.

We live in Fayetteville, Arkansas, love Scripture, and work together as business partners. Our companies and colleagues do work in organizational consulting and publishing. We have a passion to understand biblical principles that apply to work.

Book Introduction

Character matters.

Personality helps. Drive and focus make a difference. Passion plays a part. Training and education certainly make their contribution. But don't go to work without character. As a matter of fact, don't hire someone who doesn't have proven character. Don't partner with another business, either downstream or upstream, that doesn't have people of character. Don't build your best friendships with people who are bankrupt of sound, sturdy, good character. Why?

Because character matters.

This book will help establish what character is, reveal where character is developed, and then portray a series of snapshots of character on display.

Definition of Character

The sum of my behaviors,
public and private,
consistently arranged
across the spectrum
of my life.

"He chose David...to be the shepherd of his people Jacob.... And David shepherded them with integrity of heart" (Psalm 78:70-72).

CONTENTS

CHAPTER ONE

What Character Looks Like

Most of the world thought they had lost a treasured businessman of international repute when Armand Hammer died in December of 1990. He had built Occidental Petroleum into a worldwide powerhouse, and as chairman of the board, he consummated deals while globe-trotting in his private Boeing 727 jet.

He was known as a personal adviser to almost all United States presidents from Franklin D. Roosevelt to George Bush. His Rolodex listed virtually every government head in every country of significance, including the Communist nations that were out-of-bounds to United States citizens during the Cold War era. He enjoyed the company of Prince Charles of Great Britain. He cut exclusive business deals with Lenin, Brezhnev, Gorbachev, and other leaders of the Soviet Union. He purchased an interest in Arm & Hammer Baking Soda because its name coincided with his own. He won lucrative oil contracts in Qaddafi's Libya. His airplane crisscrossed the globe constantly, touching down in countries like Iran and Iraq, Nigeria, and China. He collected some of the best art in the world. He sponsored conferences on peace and human rights. Armand Hammer may literally have known more world leaders across a wider spectrum of countries and over a greater span of years than any other human being of his era.

It seems that Armand Hammer's life turned out to be ninety-two years of a carefully crafted charade. From the earliest years of his association with the Soviet Union, he funneled money into a vast Soviet spy network in the United States. Many of his companies were primarily fronts that allowed him to launder money for the Soviet regime. Hoover's FBI investigated him. He bought politicians around the world. Bribes and illegal secret deals brought him many of his business contracts.

Hammer used and discarded wives and numerous other women. In one case he arranged for his mistress of the moment to have plastic surgery and change her name so that his wife would not suspect an affair. His father went to jail twice for crimes that Armand had committed. He built one entire business on selling fake art that unsuspecting customers all over the United States thought were genuine articles from the Faberge and Romanoff treasures in Russia. He fathered children whom he would not acknowledge and whom he tried to hide. His last wife accused him of defrauding her of her wealth, and after she died, her estate sued him for $440 million. His own son refused to attend his father's funeral.

Armand Hammer's life was a torrid and tangled mess of promises not kept, obligations not met, and corruption left unchecked. His major problem—he had bad character.[1]

It's engraved in everyone.

Everyone has character, and it can be described: Bad. Good. Weak. Sturdy. Dark. Sterling. Psalm 78:72 sums up David's character as "integrity of heart." The Old Testament concept of integrity is one of "wholeness" and "blamelessness." A person of integrity, according to the Old Testament understanding, is a "what you see on the outside is what you get on the inside" individual. A man of authenticity and transparency. Someone who lives out in action what he believes in his head. A man of integrity is a "whole" person, the opposite of a two-faced hypocrite.

David, in the Old Testament, is a good example of setting and raising the character standard. Despite some serious sins with Bathsheba and her husband, Uriah, for example, the way he dealt with his relationship to God and people—even the way he dealt with his own sins—gives us a picture of, as the Scriptures describe him, a man after God's own heart.

Character comes from the Greek word describing a marking and engraving instrument. The picture is of an artist who wears a groove on a metal plate by repeatedly etching in the same place with a sharp tool. My character is forged as a set of distinctive marks that, when taken together, draw a portrait of who I really am.

It's based on behavior.

Behavior and character are linked together, but they are not the same thing. Behavior is what I do, one action at a time. "I behaved badly in that situation." Character is the sum of all my behavior, both public and private, arranged as patterns across the entire spectrum of my life. Any behavior, duplicated and reduplicated, forms a part of my character.

Repeated patterns of behavior wear a series of grooves, which, when put all together, form a portrait of me as a person or show a picture of my character. Sometimes that portrait is compelling and attractive; sometimes it is ugly and repelling. Usually it is a combination of the two. Even great faces have wrinkles and warts.

Governing my character is very different from knowing my gift mix and internal wiring (see *A Case for Calling*, Addington and Graves). Those were built into me by God when He created me. I am gifted and wired to be able to do certain things incredibly well; I have a bent towards some activities and against others; I am attracted to certain tasks and repelled by others. No matter how hard I work at improving my ability in certain areas, I may never be able to do them as well as someone else who is gifted and wired for those situations.

However, I have control over my character. I can improve it, change it, modify it, and compromise it. In a world where we seem to have little control, we call the shots when it comes to whether or not our character is diminished. Job said to his friends concerning his character: "I will not deny my integrity. I will maintain my righteousness and never let go of it; my conscience will not reproach me as long as I live" (Job 27:5-6). If my character goes down, I am the only one who can be blamed. No other person apart from me can allow my character to be compromised.

It's built over time.

Character comes in bits and pieces, not as a complete package. David's character was forged over many years and at least

four careers. It came with time, and it came in parts, not all at
once. Early in his career he was very quick to take offense and
revenge. When Nabal refused to feed David and his men in 1
Samuel 25, David's hair-trigger response to the four hundred
soldiers under his command was: "Put on your swords!" Nabal
would have died an ugly death had his wife, Abigail, not personally intervened and begged David to leave her husband
alone.

Contrast that event with one much later in David's king-
ship. During a very difficult time in David's reign over Israel,
when his own son had conspired to steal the throne, a man
named Shimei cursed David as the king fled from his palace
and the city of Jerusalem. Second Samuel 16 gives a record of
the incident:

> As he cursed, Shimei said, "Get out, get out, you man
> of blood, you scoundrel! The Lord has repaid you for
> all the blood you shed in the household of Saul, in
> whose place you have reigned. The Lord has handed
> the kingdom over to your son Absalom. You have
> come to ruin because you are a man of blood!" Then
> Abishai son of Zeruiah said to the king, "Why should
> this dead dog curse my lord the king? Let me go over

and cut off his head." But the king said, "What do you and I have in common, you sons of Zeruiah? If he is cursing because the Lord said to him, 'Curse David,' who can ask, 'Why do you do this?'" David then said to Abishai and all his officials, "My son, who is of my own flesh, is trying to take my life. How much more, then, this Benjamite! Leave him alone; let him curse, for the Lord has told him to. It may be that the Lord will see my distress and repay me with good for the cursing I am receiving today." So David and his men continued along the road while Shimei was going along the hillside opposite him, cursing as he went and throwing stones at him and showering him with dirt. (2 Samuel 16:7-13)

Building character is a day-by-day, lifetime commitment. As we allow the Holy Spirit to work in our lives and chip away at our character one piece at a time, we will be different men over time. Our character will improve. David's character did not look the same before as it did after.

It's tested over time.

We have been in business together for seven years. At the very beginning of our association, we laid out common core values to help define our relationship with each other as well as define the behavior of our organization. Those values include statements such as "We will improve each other" and "We will finish well."

We are very different men today than we were seven years ago. Our characters have been tested. They have improved. In the context of our work world, we have confronted, and in some cases continue to confront, issues such as controlling anger, keeping promises, treating colleagues as valued assets, and telling the truth. We deal with our egos and defensiveness, our ambition and stress.

Our work world is a laboratory for the improvement of our character. Every work situation is. It is often not easy. But it is always valuable.

Every single day of our work lives we take hundreds of actions. We make behavior choices scores of times. When we sum up all of those individual behaviors over an hour, then a day, then a week, then a month, then a decade, we have patterns of behavior. Those patterns of behavior make up our character.

CHAPTER TWO

How Character Is Built

I was busy working my "to do" list. It was a Monday afternoon, and my secretary said my wife was on the line. In our office we have an agreement that family calls are always pushed through—regardless. That brief phone call on that Monday afternoon shook me to the very center of my life. One of my good friends had suddenly been diagnosed with multiple myeloma, a serious form of cancer. He is my age and has four boys all still at home. He and his wife are both physicians. He is a man after God's heart. We go to church together, and our kids attend school together. Just last Friday night we had huddled together in warm blankets to watch a cold Arkansas high school football game.

Since that day, I have spent a lot of time with him. God had clearly called me to come alongside him. I thought it was so I could be of help to him during this perilous journey. However, after my first encounter, I realized that I was the beneficiary of the relationship, not my friend. God wanted to teach me something, not him. He and his family were helping me. They were helping me understand that a man's character is built day by day, decision by decision, over the years.

We cannot grow character through a crash-course weekend seminar when one day we suddenly realize we need some. It's impossible. We can't become an astronaut, or a world-class fly fisherman, or an expert brick mason in a microwave weekend of learning.

This encounter caused me to ask the question, "From where does this kind of character come?" I began to reflect deeper than I had in a long time on the issue of a man and his character. When and how had this friend of mine, his wife, and even his children developed such strong, sturdy, personal, and family character? From where does good character come?

Good character is built on a good heart.

Jesus, as He was developing a team of leaders, taught it this way, "No good tree bears bad fruit, nor does a bad tree bear good fruit. The good man brings good things out of the good stored up in his heart, and the evil man brings evil things out of the evil stored up in his heart" (Luke 6:43, 45).

A friend of mine used to say that when a man gets squeezed, whatever is in him will come out. Work has a way of squeezing a man. From those pressure points come our reflexes and reactions. It is our reflexes and reactions that publicize what is in our heart.

In the last couple of years I've observed a number of men who received the dreadful communication that their job would be changing, and sometimes the change was to be dramatic. For instance, one of my friends found out the week before Christmas that the following Friday would be his last day with his company. This man had been with his company a long time. He had poured his talents into the company, and the company had rewarded him well in the past. But suddenly those at the top felt it would be financially and strategically shrewd to "lose a couple of layers and dissolve two departments." Robert's job was gone.

He called me, and we met for a quick lunch as he replayed the story. I remember saying to him, "So, Robert, what are you going to do?"

He looked back with a little hesitation and said, "I'm going to take about a week and do some 'heart work.'"

To that, I asked, "What do you mean?"

He said, "I want to make sure I learn what I need to learn in this situation. I want to make sure that this situation makes me a better man, not a bitter man. I don't want to rationalize away some of the feedback points, nor do I want to build a wall of resentment and revenge toward my company and my boss. And, most of all, I want to make sure that I guard myself from a quick reflex of 'I've got to go out and fix my problem.' I want to make sure that I am genuinely trusting the Lord as I clean up my resume—which I haven't done in almost twenty years—and start knocking on doors."

That's character. That's a good heart.

Integrity doesn't just happen. It is planted like a seed in a man's heart where it is watered and nourished, and day by day, year by year, it develops. Some men are "built to last." Others are not. The difference is clearly the character factor.

Our culture is enamored with leadership. It should be enamored with character. Every legitimate survey done by pollsters in the last few years consistently shows that integrity, honesty, and credibility are common characteristics of superior leaders.[1] We cannot acquire these qualities simply by reading a book on "being a leader" or listening to another speech on "successful leaders." Leaders have character that has grown from the soil of a good heart, and what is in us comes out when we do "life at work."

Therefore it is critical that a man build and protect a strong, pure heart. The heart is the seat of the inner man. It comprises such elements as feelings, desires, affections, motives, will, intellect, and principles. It is in the heart that

- We process life.
- We ponder eternity.
- We transmit heritage to our children.
- We engage in real worship.
- We filter negative emotions.
- We conquer sin cycles.
- We initiate decision making.
- We forge good character.
- We knit real friendships.
- We confirm personal significance.
- We communicate to God.

As a man's heart goes, so goes the man.

Sound character sits on a solid sense of truth.

When Paul the Apostle saw the vision of Jesus on the Damascus road, he didn't change jobs; he simply changed hearts. Instead of building pagans and fighting Christians, he switched to building Christians and fighting pagans. When Paul was on assignment in Thessalonica with a handful of believers, an interesting reference to character emerges as Paul evaluated those with whom he had come in contact: "Now the Bereans were of more noble character than the Thessalonians, for they received the message with great eagerness and examined the Scriptures every day to see if what Paul said was true" (Acts 17:11).

Sound character has to be wrapped around more than an optimistic, self-willed "I will not lie," "I will not steal," or "I will not get even." We must have truth at the core, or our convictions will unravel in times of challenge. Truth acts as an internal foundation that keeps character grounded. There must be some substance, not just style. Companies and organizations struggle with this every day.

Over the last few years, our company has helped many companies generate something called a core-values statement. Our own company's core-values statement can serve as an example.

CORNERSTONE COMPANIES CORE VALUES

How We Think:

We are overt regarding our Christian commitment and agenda.

We cultivate core competencies in both Bible and business.

We adjust our agenda to fit God's personal and super-
natural direction.

How We Work:

We under-promise and over-deliver.
We plan the work and work the plan.
We coordinate our work with all who are involved.
We upgrade our individual and collective capabilities.
We do the right thing regardless of the consequence.
We accept clients based on the potential to effect
meaningful and lasting change.

How We Behave:

We build healthy relationships.
We improve each other.
We focus on and abandon ourselves to the strengths
of others.
We work hard, play hard, and share the reward.
We finish well.

A core-values statement certainly is not the only critical
document that helps any organization become a world-class
enterprise. But it is the core-values system that prescribes

behavior for its personnel. However, we have learned that core values must belong to the individual people themselves. Values cannot be passed down as Moses did the tablets. It takes more than framing them in a plaque or putting them into a wallet card to make them operational. It takes each employee, one at a time, saying, "What do these values mean to me at my work-station?"

A boss can mandate performance, but he cannot mandate character. We trust, hope, and pray that people do the right thing when we are not there and maybe when no one at all is there. That is why some people say character is what we are in the dark. But they will not do the right thing unless they know what is right and have settled the difference in their souls.

PERSONAL CONVICTIONS

The highway for character to be expressed in a man's life begins with his having sound, solid, personal convictions. What is a conviction? "A conviction is a category of God's thinking on a particular that I wholeheartedly embrace and act upon with determination." Perhaps no biblical example has more to say about character in the workplace than Daniel. With him, we watch character in the making, and we watch character on display. From his life we learn many lessons on character and convictions.

1. *Sometimes the biggest test of our convictions comes when we are detached from our comfortable Christian subculture.* Daniel had been uprooted, transplanted, given a new name, and jerked from his environment. All external anchors had been stripped. He alone was grounded in his own convictions and character (Daniel 1:1-4).

2. *Our world will aggressively attack and challenge our Christian convictions.* Young Daniel was offered food he was not supposed to eat. He was given a new education and even had his name changed. His environment had done everything possible to soften his firm stand on right and wrong. But he didn't break. As a matter of fact, he didn't even bend (Daniel 1:5-8).

3. *The display of firm Christian convictions does not have to be obnoxious and disgusting.* Daniel didn't say, "I'm a Jew, you idiot; I can't eat your food." Instead, he balanced his convictions with his desire to have positive influence and impact. This is a difficult truth for many

Christians to accept. Not Daniel. This quality could have been the quality that enabled him to serve four different administrations (Daniel 1:9-14).

4. *Holding to clear biblical convictions always carries consequences.* A display of character starts with a man knowing in his mind what is right and wrong. It is deep-seated, personalized truth that is at the base of sound, consistent decision making, which is the steel frame for sturdy character.

One of my partners met a gentleman at a strategic planning summit our company was leading for one of our clients. My partner commented, "This is a great guy. We need to spend more time with him." I've learned that some people get worse the more we get to know them, and others just unfold depth upon depth. The more we peel back, the more we find that impresses us. This man was clearly on the deep end of the pool in his character. So, a few months later we had the occasion of spending the morning with him on the East Coast. Through the conversation that morning, we learned that the man had been financially very successful years ago. But "when the market turned," he had lost everything and ended up owing creditors more than $60 million. His testimony was that although he had struggled, he knew he had to pay back every dollar. So he constructed a pay-back plan, contacted everyone, and pledged his word to clear his debt.

Last year he made his last payment for a $20,000 debt to a small bank in the Southeast. He personally drove to the bank and handed the check to the banker, who said, "I thought you would never do this."

This modern-day Daniel said, "I didn't have a choice, it was the right thing to do. I knew it years ago, and it has never left me." Opinions are something we hold, whereas convictions are something that hold us.

Good character keeps good company.

We all know this to be true when we are young and little; we just forget that it's still true as we get older. I can remember my mom instructing me to stay away from Jimmy down the street. "He's a rotten apple," she would say. (Of course we wonder how many moms were saying that about us back then.) We all know what that means. It means the same thing that Paul meant when he said decisively, "Bad company corrupts good character" (1 Corinthians 15:33). But who cautions us of rotten apples when life graduates us to our twenties, thirties, forties, and beyond?

I sat down the other day and analyzed all the relationships in my world. I broke them down into four apple categories in honor of my mother. There were healthy apples, bruised apples, rotten apples, and poisonous apples.

The healthy apples were, of course, those people who are nutritious and refreshing. Contact with them leaves us robust, hearty, and healthy. And we hope it works both ways.

Then there are the bruised apples. A bite will not make us sick, but it doesn't contribute to our health either.

Third, there are the rotten apples. Those are the people in our lives who truly have a negative impact upon us. By constantly digesting their influence, we will get sick. It is a fact.

Finally, there are poisonous apples, for which some people have a steady appetite. They are captured in a web of friendship that is killing them. Usually those captured have a hard time seeing the destructive friendship. Others around usually see a lot more clearly than we do at this point.

Walter (not his real name) was self-employed. Even as a youngster, his entrepreneurial bent was noticed. His latest career was the launching of his own communication and advertisement company. He had landed a big first account that hurled him forward. Starting strong was never Walter's problem.

It was sometime after year four that his wife first probed and asked Walter why he was slowly changing and becoming someone different than the man she had married. His reflex response was that she was making it all up and they both were getting older. Then the kids started commenting, and finally a couple of his best friends began probing. As the story unraveled, the rotten apple was exposed. Walter had experienced a surge of growth in his third year of business, and as always, business growth takes capitalization. Walter couldn't self-fund the opportunities that lay ahead of them. And like any red-blooded American entrepreneur, he put together a "deal" to bring in some outside investors. The only criteria for his investor profile was "anyone who would give him lots of money." It turned out that he had partnered with a man who had none of Walter's values and none of Walter's convictions. Eventually, someone was going to affect someone, and in the long run, Walter was affected.

He began to use language that, until that time, his family had never heard. He began a slow unraveling on many of his best qualities—patience, kindness, and even honesty. It came to a confrontation when his wife and one his key employees called Walter's hand on his handling of the company's income tax. He was cheating, and next he was lying. Healthy relationships reinforce strong character, and unhealthy relationships deteriorate our character.

Good character is shaped under suffering.

Some things come through suffering that cannot and will not come any other way.

> I walked a mile with Pleasure,
>   She chattered all the way,
> But she left me none the wiser,
>   For all she had to say.
> I walked a mile with Sorrow,
>   And ne'er a word said she;
> But, oh, the things I learned from her
>   When Sorrow walked with me!
> —"Understanding Suffering," Robert Browning

The apostle Paul put together this flowchart, which includes both suffering and character: "We also rejoice in our sufferings, because we know that suffering produces perseverance; perseverance, character; and character, hope" (Romans 5:3-4). Most of us react when suffering hits. Some people react with denial. "This can't be happening to me," they say, burying their heads in the sand. Some people react with a kind of redirection or escapism. "I'll just go fishing all weekend, or hit 'happy hour' two hours early, or lose myself in a good book." Others are pessimists from birth. Everyone knows a couple of these people. Every time you see them, they're singing a different verse of "Nobody Knows the Trouble I've Seen." And then others respond with a shallow kind of optimism. "Well, I guess I'll just have to grin and bear it."

Tough times come to all of us. Different shapes, different sizes, different weights, but they will come. The Bible acknowledges that as a fact of life on this planet. The Epistle of James says it this way: "Consider it pure joy, my brothers, whenever you face trials of many kinds, because you know that the testing of your faith develops perseverance. Perseverance must finish its work so that you may be mature and complete, not lacking anything" (James 1:2-4). How we receive and digest suffering can become one of the greatest shapers of our character.

CHAPTER THREE

Ten Character Traits for a Godly Man

1. Maintain moral purity

If you tell the truth, you don't have to remember anything. —Mark Twain

The Promise Keepers organization constantly surveys its constituents for the purpose of sharpening their emphasis to positively impact our culture. At the end of the Promise Keepers' 1996 conference season, Christian men in America responded when asked, "What one topic do you need specific help in?" The greatest response was, "Pornography or sexual purity." The struggle continues.

Two of my friends travel a lot with their work. They are seasoned veterans of the road. They are also seasoned veterans of long and faithful marriages. Those two claims many times have trouble coexisting. Most of our consultants spend six to seven nights a month on the road. We are always thinking about the potential problem, trying to protect against moral failure. Consequently, I asked my road-veteran friends to share how they have remained faithful for all these years.

"No magic formula," they said, "but we have instituted a few practical 'hedges' around our heart, our mind, and our world." Here is how one of them answered:

Hedge #1: I have a group of men back home ask the hard questions, regularly probing for fractures in my mental or emotional armor.

Hedge #2: I try to have the movie channels in the hotel rooms disconnected in the room before I ever get there.

Hedge #3: I exercise or read a book while on a road trip.

Hedge #4: I carry lots of pictures of my wife and kids and make them a part of my road conversations with clients, friends, and even strangers.

Hedge #5: I work hard to avoid being alone with female clients at night.

Hedge #6: I always share every part of my itinerary with my secretary, my wife, and my "Gestapo" accountability team.

Hedge #7: I don't give way to the smallest temptation— no innocent baby steps toward evil.

Hedge #8: I have a group of guys back home ask the hard questions, regularly probing for fractures in my mental or emotional armor. (He knew he was repeating this hedge, but he repeated it anyway. He said these hedges are the bookends.)

I asked, "Does this really work?" to which they said, "Look, if a guy wants to cheat on his wife, he will find a way to do that. It's like your income taxes. There are general structures and guidelines that help a good man to stay good, but if a good man is determined to go bad and, in this case, cheat on his taxes, he will do it. Simply because we have forms to fill out, and an April 15 deadline every year doesn't prohibit anyone from cheating."

Moral purity starts with a firm, rigid commitment to a clean heart and a clean mind. If a man works on that and then adds some practical, useful "hedges," there is a good chance he'll stay out of the ditch.

Lust is not noticing that a woman is sexually attractive. Lust is born when we turn a simple awareness into a preoccupied fantasy. When we invite sexual thoughts into our minds and nurture them, we have passed from simple awareness into lust. Martin Luther put it this way: "We cannot help it if birds fly over our head. It is another thing if we invite them to build a nest in our hair."[1]

2. Solicit honest feedback

> Do not think of yourself more highly than you ought. (Romans 12:3)

Jonathan had just received a promotion. He had worked for most of his career with the same company. His boss had received a huge promotion and would be relocating to the home office in Chicago, which would position Jonathan to manage a huge piece of the business. As a matter of fact, he would have nine directors reporting to him. He decided his first piece of business would be to sit down with the people he had been working with for the last seven years and solicit feedback on how he could improve as he moved to his new assignment. In my company, we call that kind of behavior "walking toward the barking dog." Is there a better way to get honest feedback than to ask for it?

I remember a scene four years ago when my oldest daughter was about to go into the second grade. We were in Destin, Florida, vacationing with friends. My oldest daughter and I had awakened early, so we took a hand-holding walk down the silent, still beach as we watched the sun coming up on the surf. During the walk I determined to solicit some feedback. Who better to give me a scorecard on being a daddy than my seven-year-old daughter? I took a deep breath, swallowed twice, and said, "What do you think Daddy needs to do to be a better daddy?"

She looked up ... and told me!

Whether it is feedback from a boss, an employee, a co-worker, or a six-year-old daughter, honesty sometimes hurts. But without honesty we are all reduced to an existence that teeters between hypocrisy and self-deception. Tom Peters, the American management guru, emphasized this in his best-selling book *Thriving on Chaos*. He entitles section 7 "Becoming Obsessed with Listening."[2] Although Peters was primarily emphasizing a company's need to solicit and respond to honest consumer feedback, I think the principle can still be applied to the individual. Do I want to engage in a lifetime of learning and self-improvement? Honest, objective, untarnished feedback from others is one of the surest instruments for personal growth. But it takes character to solicit feedback.

Sam Walton's success has been analyzed and praised. However, analysts on the outside oftentimes formulize Wal-Mart's success differently than the 670,000 associates on the inside. Mr. Sam consistently made trips to solicit input from his national team. He constantly asked the "What's broken" question and "What can we do about it?" Those wearing the Wal-Mart badge today smile in memory of Mr. Sam's genuine solicitation of their contribution to building Wal-Mart.

Gaining feedback requires listening. It's a skill that must be developed. Many people don't listen because they would rather speak. Many people don't listen because they have trained themselves to hear only praise. Many people don't listen because they are too busy. And many people don't listen because they don't know how to.

Soliciting feedback requires a hunger for truth and growth that only exists in the heart of character.

3. Practice real forgiveness and receive real forgiveness

Everyone says forgiveness is a lovely idea until he has something to forgive. —C.S. Lewis

My friend and I were sitting next to each other in a hot, tired gym watching our daughters play basketball. Another man came up and introduced himself to me; we chatted for a while and then he walked on down to the other end of the gym to where his daughter was practicing. My friend asked, "Do you know that guy's story?"

I said, "No, but I'd love to hear it."

He then unfolded the story that the hand-shaking stranger had stolen well over $200,000 from his employer a number of years ago. He had been caught and had gone to prison. He served his time, was released, and has returned as a refurbished part of the American workforce.

I immediately personalized the experience as I reflected back on the injuries done to me when someone had stolen from our company. I was reminded of how hard it is to forgive others when they intentionally injure us. In his book *Forgive and Forget,* Lewis Smedes says:

Only hurts that are personal, unfair, and deep require forgiveness. Slight defeats and annoyances do not require forgiveness because there was no intentional betrayal, disloyalty, or brutality involved. Forgiveness is a spiritual surgery, cutting away the wrong so the person can be seen without it. Something like peeling an orange. Forgiveness is not forgetting, excusing, smoothing things over or accepting. Quieting troubled waters is not the same as rescuing drowning people.[3]

Most work environments are staged with people, not just machinery. When people are involved, there will be mistakes and there will be misunderstandings. An employee who can't forgive will develop shallow and surface relationships and eventually begin judging the motives of all of those around him.

- Did someone forget to say thanks?
- Was I passed over for a promotion?
- Did my company let me go unfairly?
- Did someone tell me they would do something and then severely under-deliver?
- Did one of my coworkers bring a terribly bad day to work with them yesterday?

- Has someone ever judged my motives to be bad
  when they really were not?
- Do I know how to say, "I'm sorry and would you
  forgive me?"
- Do I know how to say yes and really follow through
  when someone asks for forgiveness?

Forgiveness always takes a "first stepper." Someone has to initiate the action of mending a broken fence. It will not just happen. It takes character to be a forgiver and a first stepper. Without character, forgiveness migrates to become something else.

When forgiveness puts me one up, on top, in a superior place as the benefactor, the generous one, the giver of freedom and dignity, it's not forgiveness; it's an impostor. When forgiveness ends open relationships and leaves people cautious, twice shy, safely concealed, afraid to risk free, open, spontaneous living, it's not forgiveness; it is an impostor.[4]

4. Make courageous decisions

We make our decisions, and then our decisions turn around and make us. —F.W. Boreham[5]

When Nehemiah left his post as cupbearer to Artaxerxes and moved to Jerusalem to rebuild the wall, he faced significant opposition. Their enemies threatened to undo the rebuilding of the wall. Opposition runs like a thread all the way through the book of Nehemiah. As the leader, Nehemiah was forced to deal both with the opposition and with the resulting discouragement and depression among his own people. When the people rebuilding the wall were actually threatened with bodily harm, Nehemiah made a decision to arm his own people:

Therefore I stationed some of the people behind the lowest points of the wall at the exposed places, posting them by families, with their swords, spears and bows. After I looked things over, I stood up and said to the nobles, the officials and the rest of the people, "Don't be afraid of them. Remember the Lord, who is great and awesome, and fight for your brothers, your sons and your daughters, your wives and your homes." When our enemies heard that we were aware of their plot and that God had frustrated it, we all returned to the wall, each to his own work. From that day on, half of my men did the work, while the other half were

equipped with spears, shields, bows and armor....
Those who carried materials did their work with one
hand and held a weapon in the other, and each of the
builders wore his sword at his side as he worked....
Neither I nor my brothers nor my men nor the guards
with me took off our clothes; each had his weapon,
even when he went for water. (Nehemiah 4:13-23)

As a result of that decision, the wall was finished, and the
people celebrated.

Character gives a man the well to draw from to hold his
stand on a hard issue. It takes courage to make good decisions
involving hard issues over that span of a man's life. Why?
Sometimes because of the external opposition around us and
sometimes because of the doubt and fear inside us. Either
attack will prey on our decision-making skill. We can either
become paralyzed with indecision and second-guessing or we
can release decision arrows that have little chance of hitting the
intended target. The effect is a bad decision, a misguided decision, or a half-baked decision.

Finishing strong over the long haul is made possible by finishing strong at single-decision intersections. Finishing strong
hourly will lead to finishing strong daily. Finishing strong daily

will lead to finishing strong weekly. Finishing strong weekly will lead to finishing strong monthly. And finishing strong monthly will lead to finishing strong yearly, which will position a man to finish life well at his last lap.

5. Remain flexible

We cannot direct the wind, but we can adjust the sails.[6]

Scripture is full of examples of men of God who had to change their plans to fulfill God's purposes. In the book of Genesis, Joseph had to leave his home in Canaan and take up residence in Egypt. He did not want to go, but having the strength of character to remain obedient to God, he flourished in spite of the unfairness of his brothers and his Egyptian masters.

Daniel also was taken captive from Israel to Babylon, controlled by a ruthless regime. As part of God's plan, Daniel served as a high administrator under four separate rulers in two kingdoms. He ended up being highly influential, introducing kings in both the Babylonian and Medo-Persian empires to the one true God. His influence also paved the way for the return of the Jewish exiles to Jerusalem and Israel.

Nehemiah was a cupbearer, or a top aid, to King Artaxerxes. Because of the burden that God placed on Nehemiah's heart, he left a very secure, comfortable, and influential position to go to Jerusalem to rebuild the walls around that city that had been destroyed when Jerusalem was overrun and pillaged.

Joseph, Daniel, and Nehemiah were, according to Scripture, in the center of God's will in the process of moving from one context of service into another.

Most people don't like change. Change usually means pain, and, naturally, we hate to hurt. Therefore, we tend to get comfortable with business as usual. Being a change leader, change agent, and a willing follower of change is crucial to most personal and corporate success.

One of my partners and I have adopted the "four immutable laws of international travel."

1. It could turn out just like you planned.
2. It could turn out better than you planned.
3. It could turn out worse than you planned.
4. It could turn out "different" than you planned.

So also goes life. Rarely does life happen "just as we planned." It might be worse, it might be better, but it certainly is usually "different." Obviously, we would not be discounting planning. We have built a part of our business on training organizations in an integrated, strategic planning process. Planning, organization, and forethought are three expressions of God's nature that run from Genesis to Revelation. Our trouble is that once we have a plan, we curl up and get comfortable with it. And many times that produces a passive, nonengaged bystander in life.

"Many are the plans in a man's heart, but it is the Lord's purpose that prevails" (Proverbs 19:21).

6. Practice good time management

Make the best use of your time.[7]

The other day, one of our consultants said to me, "It's shocking how much wasted time or misdirected time exists in many corporations and organizations." He had just helped a company clarify roles and tasks among its management team. To do that, he had asked everyone to track their time for a couple of weeks, and then turn in the logbook. Not long after that, I heard a foreman who runs a framing crew for a local builder say, "Most workers ought to reimburse their employers 15 to

30 percent of their check every two weeks, because of their slippery, sloppy handling of time."

Time management is really a misnomer because we all have exactly the same amount of time, although some accomplish several times as much as others do with their time. Self-management is a better term because it implies that we manage ourselves and the time allotted us.[8]

The key is not simply to push harder on the pedal. To maximize the time God has given us to steward, we can't be obsessed with only revving up the rpm's. We have to become obsessed with character.

Our time is a gift, and our time is not our own! We didn't carve it out for ourselves, and rarely do we spend fifteen minutes when we are the only ones impacted if time is marginalized, misused, or squandered.

There is a delicate balance between being busy and being productive. Peter Senge in *The Fifth Discipline* establishes the case that effective workers "think and learn, not just go and do."[9] There is also a delicate balance between being available and being flexible, with being focused and being efficient. Building people is time-consuming. It always has been and always will be. Ask any effective mom or dad or ask any effective people builder. Thinking strategically is a time strangler. Reflection and evaluation can be a time burner.

Effective time management starts not on the Franklin or Day-Timer "to do" list but in the mind and heart of a man's character.

The supply of time is totally inelastic. No matter how high the demand, the supply will not go up. Time is also totally perishable and cannot be stored. Yesterday's time is gone forever and will never come back. And lastly, time is totally irreplaceable. Within limits, we can substitute one resource for another, but there is no substitute for time.[10]

7. Handle money correctly

Money is amoral, neutral, just like a handgun or morphine. Put a pistol in a hand of a policeman and it's a tool for justice. But in the hand of a criminal, it is an instrument of evil. —Pat Morely[11]

The story was almost too much for me to believe. The man had lost his wallet with all of his credit cards and important personal identification. But, as luck would have it, he had also just cashed his weekly $450 check and put all of the money in the back of his wallet.

He and his wife both worked, and every dollar was already accounted for. Each dollar had a temporary envelope at home that would regulate spending for the next seven days. The rest of the evening went terrible (as one might expect) as he and his wife lamented their loss and with anxious hearts tried to figure out what to do.

The next morning his doorbell rang. There stood two teenage boys holding his wallet, relating where they had found it. Being grateful, the man thought, "Well, maybe at least I can recover my driver's license and other identification." As he opened his wallet, to his shock, all of his credit cards were still there. And as he folded the back open, he noticed that all of his money was also still intact. Not one dollar was missing.

The man thought, "This must be an angel encounter." No pair of teenage boys in America would take the time on Saturday morning, hunt down a stranger, and return $450 in cash. The local newspaper did an interview, and even the reporter sat in disbelief as she asked the two boys, "Why did you return all of that cash?"

In response, one of the boys smiled and said, "Because it wasn't ours and it belonged to someone else."

Still struggling, the reporter continued, "Didn't you want to keep the money at all?"

These two young lads had character. It's too bad there is not a place on a resume to put this kind of life experience. For sure, I know a lot of companies that would love to have that quality of fiscal responsibility engrafted into each person on their payroll.

There are so many ditches a man can fall into regarding money! Handling money correctly can be like successfully walking from one side of a zoo to another after someone lets all of the animals out of their cages. The dangers and difficulties with money come in so many different forms of attack.

- Do I frivolously spend or unwisely invest what I make?
- Do I handle my company's money as precisely and scrupulously as I do my own?
- Do I ascribe personal value to income level?
- Are my expense reports true and accurate?
- Do I only relate to one economic slice of our society and practice discrimination against the others?
- Are my views about money too rigid, legalistic, and conservative?
- Are my views about money too loose, liberal, and slippery?

- Am I a slave to indebtedness and spending habits?
- Am I obsessed with money whether I have a lot or a little?
- Do I consider my job only as valuable as my pay-check?

It takes a man of character to handle money correctly. What should I do? View it balanced. Hold it loosely. Manage it wisely.

8. Weather unfairness and injustice

The same heat that melts the butter hardens the clay.[12]

A number of years ago I almost lost my life in a terrible truck accident. It was an early winter morning, and I was at the wheel of a truck, driving west on the so-called Chicago Skyway, which is an eighteen-mile toll bridge that connects the Indiana Tollway with the Chicago Loop. The roads were slippery because of the inordinate amount of snow that had fallen that winter. When a car ahead of me began to slow down, I braked, and immediately the truck went violently out of control. I slid through the median into the eastbound lane and over the edge of the bridge. My tractor-trailer fell sixty feet onto a road that

•

ran alongside the bridge. Although it took Chicago firemen more than an hour to cut me out of my mangled vehicle, I was miraculously spared serious injury.

The company for whom I drove fired me. I ended up in the hospital, with a long recovery ahead of me, and without a job. I found out soon after the accident that the reason the truck had gone out of control was that the brakes on the steering axle had actually been disconnected by mechanics who couldn't figure out how to adjust them properly.

Injustice and unfairness are standard parts of our lives, and will be until Jesus comes again. All the way through the Old and New Testaments are examples of men who all their lives had to endure unfair treatment. None are more dramatic than the Old Testament story of a godly businessman named Job. His life opens with things going very well, only to have the bottom continuously drop out. He was served unfairness and injustice with an intensity and consistency that would make most of us do more than just ask lots of questions.

So what is supposed to be our response to unfairness and injustice?

First, don't become cynical and skeptical. Many times a series of unfair experiences will leave us riddled with a long list of negative feelings and expressions, such as "There is really no good that will ever happen or can happen to me" or "A good God doesn't exist and certainly does not have good intentions for me." Or we may begin to construe the notion that everyone in the world has a devious, dangerous agenda for us. George Maraneth, a nineteenth-century English novelist, observed, "Cynics are only happy in making the world as barren to others as they have made it for themselves."[13]

Second, don't become hardened and judgmental. Unfairness and injustice drive many people to bestow upon themselves the responsibility of judging other people's behavior and motives. That self-assignment carries at least two hazards. First, it is God's job to judge, not ours. Second, we rarely have all of the facts connected to any situation. Therefore, we should guard against becoming judgmental in times of unfairness.

Third, don't become resistant and disbelieving. Men who have been burned easily become distrustful of anyone, anytime, for anything. They insert another layer of barrier between them and friends, and even between them and their own healthy attitudes. They live the life of a doubting Thomas, which can become a very negative influence on any work team.

9. Fail without failing

A failure is not someone who has tried and failed; it is someone who has given up trying and resigned himself to failure; it is not a condition, but an attitude.
—Sydney J. Harris

When we think of David in the Bible, we obviously think of a very successful king—a man whose life was aligned after God's own heart. But our viewpoint of his career is always from the end looking back. It ended well. He was very successful. However, the word *successful* is not always the word we would attach to every snapshot of his personal and professional life. Some of his life was spent in situations of failure. David was a convicted murderer, adulterer, and fugitive. Yet at the end of his career, God was willing to evaluate his motives and performance by proclaiming, "David was a man after mine own heart."

The cover story of *Fortune* magazine (May 1, 1995) was titled "So You Fail. Now Bounce Back!" It was a story that chronicled the failure and recovery of twenty key American executives. Among the lessons was that debacles and disasters will happen. Such experience is common to all. What is not common is how we weather those storms and quakes and how life turns out.[14]

The difference is clearly the character factor. One could argue, "If a man had such good character in the first place, why did he fail and falter?" That case can be argued. However, the question is not how to minimize our failures, which could have been another study, but rather how to handle failure when it occurs. Character doesn't look for someone to blame. It doesn't try to relabel the failure to something more appealing as the cause. It doesn't throw in the towel of confidence and hope and accept defeat. It squares up its shoulders, like David did in Psalm 51, and admits to full or partial participation. It analyzes enough to extract principles for future improvement. It might try to fix the problem, or it might simply say, "I'm sorry, please forgive me." And then it focuses on the future, not the past, and moves on.

10. Successfully handle success

Looks aren't everything.
  Luxury is not everything.
Money is not everything.
  Health is not everything.
Success is not everything.
  Happiness is not everything.
Even everything is not everything.
  There's more to life than everything.[15]

"Success means attaining some measure of money, fame, power, and self-fulfillment—and then looking the part."[16] That is the way one man defined it. For certain, our culture sees success as synonymous with achievement and accomplishment. Success tests a man's character more accurately than failure. It lays bare our motivations and puts a body on our theology.

Recently I received a phone call from a friend candidating for a COO position in a $100 million company. He is a battle-trained veteran of business. He told me he was thinking of withdrawing his name from the recruiters' short list. His reason was that the founder/CEO seemed to be drunk on his own success. Sometimes that attitude appears as a self-involved one-way conversation. Sometimes it appears as false humility, constantly saying, "We're not sure why we're successful; we're just doing our best."

So, what is a successful man supposed to think, and how should he act regarding his own success?

1. *Be careful not to ever let success rearrange the order of the universe.* We are not the center of the universe. We are not even a planet. Each of us is one person, residing on one planet. Sometimes success has a way of rearranging all of the components of our universe. That would make for a humorous map to be stretched across the office wall.

2. *Be careful not to ever let success be defined or measured without the God factor.* Ronald Reagan used to tell a story about two fellows who were out hiking in the woods and suddenly looked up and saw a grizzly bear coming over the hill toward them. One of them immediately reached into his pack, pulled out a pair of sneakers, and started removing his boots and putting on the sneakers. The other one standing there said, "You don't think you can outrun that grizzly, do you?" And the first one said, "I don't have to, I just have to

be able to outrun you." For many people, success is only defined and measured in the horizontal. "It is my performance against yours." Certainly that performance comparison can be of some help to guide continuous improvement. But success must have a vertical component also. There is the God factor. A man of character realizes this and religiously blends God's role into all his achievements.

3. *Be careful not to ever think that past success continually means future success.* One of the biggest dangers of success is an arrogance of presumption that can cultivate in the hardened mind of the successful. The story is told of the man who went to his boss's office one Monday morning. His boss gave him a $50 bill and said, "I just want you to know how good of a job you did this last week." The next Monday the same thing happened. The next Monday the same thing, and the next Monday the same thing. On the fifth week, the boss didn't call. The worker was furious, called his wife, and threatened to quit. It is so easy for us to lose a tight grip on the slippery emotion of arrogance and presumption.

Conclusion

I f every Christian man would evidence sterling, sturdy character in the workplace, a chain reaction of evangelism would result. The non-Christians in our work world need the words and actions of Christianity to be melded within one person. We must display good character; then we may begin telling the good news of Jesus Christ. Character matters.

So it was with David the shepherd, the musician, the soldier, and the king. So it is with all of us. A life without character will unravel. To be honest, it might not come apart until after we are gone, like Armand Hammer, but it will be exposed. But the good news is that the same principle applied to David's life. God saw David as a man with a heart of wholeness or integrity who pleased Him across the span of his life. Now there is a hero worth following!

Where Do I Go from Here?

1. *Pray.*

   Don't try to make improvements on your character without God. Carve out a few minutes every day and discuss your "character condition" with the Lord.

2. *Ask.*

   Have three talks soliciting feedback on your character. Ask your spouse, ask your children, and ask a friend to help you honestly gauge your character development.

3. *Identify.*

   Put your finger on two specific facets of your character that could use an overhaul. Write down your goal on a three-by-five-inch card and keep it with you for thirty days. Go ahead and list out some strategies that will help you achieve your goal.

4. *Read.*

   With a pen in hand, read through either Daniel's or Nehemiah's life in the Old Testament looking for examples of positive character development.

5. *Assess.*

   Do a quick assessment of the relationships in your life, and define which are constructive towards positive character development and which are destructive.

6. *Share.*

   Find a circle of friends to share with. Add the sharp edge of accountability to your good intentions.

7. *Give.*

   Make sure you're not trying to grow a clean life from a dirty heart. Give your life to Christ if you've never done that.

Notes

Chapter One

1. Edward J. Epstein, *Dossier: The Secret History of Armand Hammer* (New York: Random House, 1996).

Chapter Two

1. James M. Kouzes and Barry Z. Posner, *Leadership Challenge* (San Fransisco: Jossey-Bass Publishers, 1987), pp. 17-19.

Chapter Three

1. Pat Morley, *Man in the Mirror: Solving the Twenty-Four Problems Men Face* (Nashville: Thomas Nelson Publishers, Inc., 1992), p. 262.
2. Tom Peters, *Thriving on Chaos* (New York: Vintage Books, a Division of Random House, 1987).
3. "Smedes, Larson Highlight Scholars Week," *Southwestern News,* April 1983, p. 7.
4. David Augsburg, *Caring Enough to Forgive* (Ventura, California: Regal Books, 1981), p. 8.

5. Sherwood Wirt and Kersten Beckstrom, *Topical Encyclopedia of Living Quotations* (Minneapolis, Minnesota: Bethany House Publishers, 1982), p. 50.

6. Edyth Draper, *Draper's Book of Quotations for the Christian World* (Wheaton, Illinois: Tyndale House Publishers, Inc., 1992).

7. J. B. Phillips, *Letters to Young Churches* (New York: The Macmillan Company, 1958), p. 108.

8. Stephen Covey, *Principle-Centered Leadership* (New York: Fireside: Simon & Schuster, Inc., 1992), p. 137-8.

9. Peter Senge, *The Fifth Discipline* (New York: Bantam/Doubleday, 1994).

10. Peter F. Drucker, *The Effective Executive* (New York: Perinnial Library, Harper & Row, 1966, 1967), pp. 25-26.

11. Morely, p. 133.

12. Draper.

13. Daniel Taylor, *Cynicism* (Downers Grove, Illinois: InterVarsity, 1982), p. 5.

14. Patricia Sellers, "So You Fail. Now Bounce Back!" *Fortune*, 1 May 1995.

15. Steve Turner and Dennis Haack, *The Rest of Success* (Nashville: Thomas Nelson Publishers, Inc., 1991), p. 50.

16. Ibid., p. 40.

A CASE FOR
Serving

Also by ™Life@Work Co.™

A Case for Calling
A Case for Character
A Case for Skill

A CASE FOR
Serving

Discovering the Difference a Godly Man Makes in His Life at Work

DR. STEPHEN GRAVES & DR. THOMAS ADDINGTON

Cornerstone *Alliance*

FAYETTEVILLE, ARKANSAS 72702

Published by Cornerstone Alliance
Post Office Box 1928
Fayetteville, AR 72702

ISBN 1-890581-03-8

Cover design by Sean Womack of Cornerstone Alliance.

Printed in the United States of America

1 3 5 7 9 10 8 6 4 2

To our wives

Karen and Susan

*who have modeled serving
as a day-to-day way of life.*

Series Introduction

Our offices are on the fourth floor of the second tallest building in northwest Arkansas. We have an extraordinary view of the rolling hills of Fayetteville from our panoramic picture windows. Although our city is growing, it still has the feel of a small town. Almost everyone knows almost everyone.

From that vantage point we enjoy watching cycles of life unfold around us. Unlike some parts of the country, we benefit from the whole assortment of seasons. The snowy mantle of winter melts into the sweaty heat of summer, with all variations in between.

We also watch the daily routine of hundreds of businesses. At the start of a day we can see the lights of other businesses coming on, like eyes popping open after a good night's sleep. At the end of a day we witness those same lights going out. The next morning it begins all over again. Then again. Then again.

We talk to many men for whom that description sums up their work experience. People come and go; accounts open and close. Creditors get paid; customers get billed. We pick up; we deliver. We punch in; we punch out. The workday begins, then ends. We earn our money; we spend our money. The cycle is unrelenting and unending. Then the cycle quits, and we die.

Is that all there is? Is routine drudgery what a man should expect from his work life and career?

What is the difference in the behavior and experience of a Christian man in his work compared to that of a non-Christian man?

What does it mean to be a Christian who practices dentistry? Does it mean that I have Bible verses on my business card? Do I share Christ with patients while they are under anesthesia? Or perhaps I ought to treat only Christian patients. If someone doesn't pay me, should I send their bill into collections, or should I forgive the debt and maybe pay for it myself? Should I work longer hours to display an incredible work ethic? Or maybe I need to work shorter hours so that I can spend more time with my family or serve on a church or community committee. Do I pay my employees more than the national average? Or do I pay them less so they can learn to live by faith?

What does it mean to be a Christian plumber? Do I cut my rates for Christian customers? Should I work on Sunday, or do I fail to respond to a crisis that comes on the Sabbath? Perhaps I need to hand out gospel tracts to other subcontractors on the job. Should I release one of my crew if he's incompetent? Or are Christians bound to keep every employee on the payroll for life? What does the Bible say about work?

A number of years ago we came across a verse in the New Testament book of Acts that serves as God's final epitaph for King David:

> When David had served God's purpose in his own generation, he fell asleep. (Acts 13:36)

Those words complete a description of David found way back in the Old Testament book of Psalms:

> He chose David his servant and took him from the sheep pens; from tending the sheep he brought him to be the shepherd of his people Jacob, of Israel his inheritance. And David shepherded them with integrity of heart; with skillful hands he led them. (Psalm 78:70-72)

David was a shepherd, a musician, a soldier, and a king. He had a very busy, full, and successful career. We would like to use those verses about David as the basis for exploring the making of a godly man in and through his work world. This short series will consist of four parts:

....David... *served God's purpose...*: A Case for Calling

      He chose *David his servant...*: A Case for Serving

....David shepherded them

        with *integrity of heart*: A Case for Character

....with *skillful hands* he led them: A Case for Skill

So, we are back to one of our questions from above. Is work basically an unending and unfulfilling cycle of activity? Answer: it depends. On what? On whether or not I know God.

According to King Solomon, one of the wisest and wealthiest men of all time:

A man can do nothing better than to eat and drink and find satisfaction in his work. This too, I see, is from the hand of God.... *To the man who pleases him, God gives wisdom, knowledge and happiness, but to the sinner he gives the task of gathering and storing up wealth to hand*

it over to the one who pleases God. (Ecclesiastes 2:24-26;
italics added)

Without God in my life, I might be driven, full of ambition, and very successful. I might even make it to the pinnacle of my profession. But I will not enjoy my work over time. It will not bring me fulfillment. I will be on a treadmill.

These books address a Christian man in the workplace. The definition and clarity that the Bible brings to a man and his work world are reserved for those who enjoy a personal relationship with Jesus. If you don't know Him, we strongly urge you to invite Him into your life. Then join us in exploring the topic of work in the incredibly rich, amazingly untapped pages of Scripture.

May the favor of the Lord our God rest upon us;
establish the work of our hands for us—
yes, establish the work of our hands. (Psalm 90:17)

A word about our writing style. As coauthors, we speak in the first person when telling a story that relates to one of us as individuals. But we do not identify who belongs to which story. To help unravel that mystery, the following are some personal characteristics that will help sort us out.

Steve is an avid fisherman who baited hooks as a young boy on the Mississippi Gulf Coast. His appetite for learning and his energy for making friends have trademarked his twenty-three years of ministry and business.

Tom grew up in Hong Kong as the son of a medical missionary. He spent a number of years driving eighteen-wheelers, and he has taught at three universities.

We live in Fayetteville, Arkansas, love Scripture, and work together as business partners. Our companies and colleagues do work in organizational consulting and publishing. We have a passion to understand biblical principles that apply to work.

Book Introduction

Serving others.

It doesn't come naturally. We are born bent in the opposite direction. Instead of having a fine-tuned radar directed outward towards other people's needs and betterment, we are usually focused on taking care of ourselves. We are skilled at arranging information, opportunities, and even relationships around a self-interested grid. "What is in it for me?" is the single criteria.

Until we meet Jesus...the One who cast aside what was good for Him and acted upon what was good for us. He broke the grip that self-centeredness has on all of us. He taught serving to others. He modeled serving among others. He was...the Suffering Servant...for me...for all of us.

It still doesn't come naturally every time, but as a Christian I can learn and develop the art of selfless living.

This book will help establish what serving is, reveal what makes serving so difficult, and then portray a series of snapshots of serving being modeled.

Definition of Serving

The art of focusing
on someone else's interest
instead of my own.

"He chose David his servant and took him from the sheep-pens....he brought him to be the shepherd of his people" (Psalm 78:70-71).

CONTENTS

CHAPTER ONE

What Serving Is

The philosophy of "me first" has the power to blow our world to pieces, whether applied to marriage, business, or international politics. —James C. Dobson[1]

Albert Nobel left most of his fortune in a trust. Since 1901 the Nobel Foundation headquartered in Stockholm, Sweden, has been awarding annual prizes to those individuals who have marked our globe with an exceptional humanitarian effort.

Alfred Bernhard Nobel was born into a family of inventors and early entrepreneurs. His family had been manufacturing nitroglycerin when an explosion in 1864 killed five people, including Alfred's younger brother, Emil. Searching for a safer way to handle nitroglycerin, Nobel worked tirelessly until he concocted a way to pack the explosion into another material, which greatly reduced its volatility. In 1867, thirty-four-year-old Alfred Nobel patented and introduced dynamite to the world. Of his 355 patents, it would be his most famous and by far his most lucrative. The discovery of dynamite would become the funding backbone for Nobel Prizes. The average prize has grown from about $30,000 to about $825,000 in 1993. The list of recipients is an impressive parade of discoveries and advancements around the world.

- 1901—Jean H. Dunant (Switzerland), for his work at organizing the Geneva conventions of 1863 and 1864, which led to the establishment of the International Red Cross.

- 1906—Theodore Roosevelt (USA), for his mediation of the Russo-Japanese war and his intervention between Britain, France, and Germany concerning Morocco.

- 1952—Albert Schweitzer (France), for his efforts on behalf of the Brotherhood of Nations.

- 1964—Martin Luther King, Jr. (USA), for his efforts to bring about integration within the United States without violence.

- 1973—Henry A. Kissinger (USA), for his work in negotiating an end to the war in Vietnam.

• 1978—Menachem Begin (Israel), for his contribution to the two frame agreements on peace in the Middle East and on peace between Egypt and Israel, which were signed at Camp David on September 17, 1978.

• 1984—Bishop Desmond Tutu (South Africa), for his work against apartheid.

• 1986—Elie Wiesel (USA), for his books and lectures on his experiences as a survivor of the Nazi concentration camps of Auschwitz and Buchenwald.

• 1990—Mikhail Gorbachev (USSR), for helping to end the cold war and the Communist order in Eastern Europe, paving the way for German unification and democratic changes.

And these are but a selected few representing the Nobel Peace Prize. Every year since 1901, exceptional service towards mankind has been recognized and awarded.

However, the undeniable common thread woven through each and every recipient has been that none had the primary goal to win the Nobel Prize or to receive worldwide fame or a huge cash payment. Their motivation was to help, care for, and serve others, not themselves—pure and untarnished interest in other people.

Few Nobel Prize winners have intrigued the world like the small, frail servant from Calcutta, India. Mother Teresa won the Nobel Peace Prize in 1979 for her work among the destitute, the dying, and the orphan children in the slums of Calcutta. Read her address slowly, deliberately, and out loud. It tells nearly all that anyone needs to know about this model of servanthood.

Born: August 27, 1910, a Roman Catholic
                missionary
Address: Missionary of Charity, Nirmal, Hriday,
                Home for Dying Destitutes, 5A
                Lower Circular Road, Calcutta, India

The word *servant* is a rich, biblical concept that conveys the idea of working for and in the direction of someone else. There are well over a thousand references to servant, serving, and service in the sixty-six books of the Bible. It is a central component of the message of Christianity. It is a quality that God emphasizes and elevates as a universal language for all who have passed beneath the cross of Christ.

But what is serving at its core? When stripped to the basics, what does it mean and what does it look like? Serving is the art and act of focusing on someone else's interest, not my own. That definition will demand a role reversal for most of us in a country and a culture where self-driven, self-deserved attention is the common currency of exchange. Any Christian who serves others as a lifestyle might find himself in line for a Nobel Peace Prize. Actually, most of us will not receive a world-recognized trophy, but every act of serving will be registered with God and felt by someone.

Serving others requires a "Copernican revolution" of sorts. Prior to 1543, even the most brilliant minds had the universe framed around the wrong center point. Going against almost every shred of science, history, and experience, Copernicus placed not the earth but the sun at the center of the universe. This revolutionary idea eventually caused all the planets and celestial bodies to be reordered accordingly by astronomers.

Each individual must undergo a Copernican reordering to become a lifetime servant. We must redraw the universe around others, not ourselves. Joe White, at Kanukkuk Camps in Branson, Missouri, calls this the "I am third" philosophy. God is first, others are second, and I am always third. As an aside, the "I am third" award is the highest recognition passed out each week in the Kanukkuk sporting-camp system.

A national magazine front cover caught my eye the other day. At the bottom of the cover was a caption that read, "Self-Centered and Proud of It." The sketch that illustrated the lead article was a large, ever-expanding balloon head, loosely tied to a tiny man's shirt collar.

Serving is the exact opposite. It is the art and act of pumping someone else up, not myself.

In the last few years, an employee-evaluation tool has worked its way through the business community. It is called a "360-degree performance audit." Essentially it is the evaluating of someone's performance based on input and feedback from all areas that surround an employee. Those over us. Those under us. Those next to us. Those we buy from. Those we sell to. Suppose your company initiated a 360-degree servanthood audit? How would you fare? How would those around score you on being interested in other people, not just yourself? Would they say that you've discovered the Copernican revolution yet?

We live in a world that might periodically consider self-lessness as a trait to be pursued. But the predominant message constantly piped in from our entire existence is, "What about me?" or "What's in it for me?" or "How about me?" When someone gets a promotion, we ask what that does to our salary. When a new strategic plan is rolled out by management, we are concerned about our workload. If the company had a bad year and earnings are down, we immediately grab a calculator and refigure our bonus.

J.B. Phillips had this to say about self-centeredness.

Christ regarded the self loving, self regarding, self seeking spirit as the direct antithesis of real living. His two fundamental rules for life were that "love energy", instead of being turned in on itself should go out first to God, and then to other people.[1]

So is serving risky? Yes it is.

- It means getting to know people as people, not just human work machines.
- It means learning their names, their spouses, their parents, and maybe even their kids' ages and birthdays.
- It means getting involved with people, not always keeping a professional distance.
- It means becoming a good listener, not just a good talker.

- It means asking more questions and then really standing still, looking at them in the eyes, and listening to their response.
- It means remembering the conversations.
- It means taking the time to figure out how I can affirm someone else, get someone else promoted, get someone else's project funded, not just my own.

Regardless of my occupation, my title, or even my function, if I work around people, I can model serving. And get ready, because people hurt, people have emotions, people need direction, and people need leadership. And serving means focusing on someone else's interest, not my own. So how do we know if we are serving others? Robert Greenleaf in the book *On Becoming a Servant-Leader* takes a look from the other side of serving with these words:

Do those being served grow as persons: do they, while being served, become healthier, wiser, freer, more autonomous, more likely themselves to become servants? And what is the effect on the least privilege in society; will she or he benefit, or, at least, be not further deprived?[2]

Our business has grown every year since we started. The managing partner of our consulting firm likes to say we never have an opening, but we are always hiring. One of the joys of growing a business for us has been the prospect of building a long-term, high-performance team that is very business intensive and very ministry intensive.

The other day a new resume made its way to my in-box. The guy was impressive. Incredible credentials. Fantastic education. Unreal achievements. Off-the-chart life experiences. The more I read, the more I wondered what was not recorded on his resume. For example, where would anyone be able to detect a servant's heart and a servant's spirit? And then it hit me. What kind of resume would any of us have if the only virtues and entries we could include would be the achievements and accomplishments that others around us say we have helped them attain? If my resume was based upon my ability to serve others, how attractive would I be in the workplace?

Listen to these words from *The Message* that preview a job-focus sheet of sorts for Jesus, the Servant of all servants. "Whoever wants to be great must become a servant. Whoever wants to be first among you must be your slave. That is what the Son of Man has done: He came to serve, not to be served—and then to give away his life in exchange for many who are held hostage" (Mark 10:43-45, *The Message*).

CHAPTER TWO

What Makes Serving So Difficult?

Without God, we cannot. Without us, God will not.
—Saint Augustine[1]

Some things come easily. Some come only through sweat, blood, and a set of worn-out, calloused knees. Other things seem never to come, regardless of what we do or how long we wait.

Some things are enthusiastically encouraged and fueled by our culture. Some things are allowed but not embraced. Other things collide with our culture and society like a salmon, fighting its way upstream to spawn, always against the current.

Serving others is not an easy discipline to develop, nor does our culture reward servanthood in everyday life. Yes, we pass out a prize or two a year to acknowledge huge and rare expressions of service to others. But usually we don't look for service to others to be valued in our community or to be a part of the script on television or the big screen.

Why is serving so difficult? A number of subtle pressures act as the river current to push us constantly downstream towards self-centeredness.

The modern church movement

For almost six years now, I've enjoyed a running conversation with a friend named Robert. He is the directional pastor of a very effective church in Little Rock, Arkansas.

Our discussion has centered around this question: What does it look like for a modern church to marry substance and innovation? Our initial conversation began when we both noticed a significant evolution taking place within the American modern church. Baby-boomer consumerism was alive and active in the membership rolls of the American church. The upside was that the church was still relevant. The downside was that the church had begun reengineering itself to become market driven toward its constituents, the customers. The structure began changing. Terminology began changing. Funding strategies changed. Staffing requirements and facilities changed. It seemed that any and every expression of ecclesiology was undergoing an overhaul.

So what is wrong with innovation and relevance? one might ask. Surely upgrades and face-lifts are permissible, even sometimes profitable. Yes, they are. Nothing about change is dangerous in itself. Actually, change can be a very good thing. But there were negative, unintended consequences that accompanied all of this modernization within the church. There was significant fallout.

Perhaps the most visible shift in the last two decades was the "felt-need" style of preaching that suddenly revamped most pulpits on Sundays and most homiletics classes on Monday. Suddenly any preacher who wanted to be effective and relevant started in his sermon preparation with the consumer in the pew and worked backwards to the Bible. Thus, many "growing churches" were offering a Sunday by Sunday dose of such sermons as "How to handle your money," "How to handle your emotions," and "Six steps to making your marriage successful."

What does this have to do with serving? you might ask. More than we might realize. Within the eclipse of a brief decade, many of the flagship churches in America had developed an additive level of self-interest. And it was being nourished from our pulpits. The expectation coming to church was now:

- What will I get from the message today?
- How will you help me with my problems?
- If I give dollars, what will I get back—a better building, a nicer nursery, a more professional choir leader—
  what's in it for me?

The good news was that unchurched Harry and Mary didn't know any better and they were at least being reached. The bad news was that we didn't convert Harry and Mary to *servant membership*; they converted us to *consumer membership*. We went from "What can I do to help you" to "I want it now, I want it cheap, and I want the best quality, and if I don't get what I want, I want my money back, now." Naturally it wasn't usually expressed this graphically, but the viewpoint was still predominantly "What's in it for me?" and not "What can I do to help you?"

The greatest consequence of this shift in the modern church is that many Christians suddenly had no checks and balances on their appetite toward self-involvement. If the church doesn't call us to give, not get, where will we ever receive that message? I'm glad to report that in the last two to three years there seems to be some correction taking place. As bitter as the pill might be, the church must always convert the culture, lest we be squeezed into its mold and be scored ineffective in our calling.

The American spirit of independence

No people have ever accomplished what we have in such a short period of time. We are the most self-contained, self-sufficient country in the world—or for that matter, the history of the world. Active in our bloodstream is a spirit of self-willed reliance that keeps America positioned as the lead goose, even in a flock of highly competitive birds. We can make it on our own just fine! We have since we cut the cord with the mother country, England, and we are certain we will always be the best. Just sit back and watch us.

Confidence—we have plenty for those who have none. But there is a downside to this strength. Robert Bellah, in *Habits of the Heart*, suggests that "[rugged individualism] might eventually isolate Americans one from another and thereby undermine the conditions of freedom."[2] Individualism, which in the past gave America strength, now threatens the survival of freedom itself.

At the core of individualism is the lack of accountability. The Bible, in contrast, calls us to be accountable to God and to other people. We are called to be, not rugged individualists, but members of community. We are to live in relationship to others.

To serve others effectively and to be served demand that we become interdependent. We have to become intentionally involved with other people. *Webster's Collegiate Dictionary* defines *involve* as "to engage as a participant; to occupy (as oneself) absorbingly; to relate closely; to connect; or to include." If I am to be a model of serving, I must become involved with other people. I must see it as my responsibility to help others, as well as allow others to help me.

Pass the ego biscuits, please

My kids acquired a guinea pig through an informal neighborhood negotiation between my wife and a friend's wife. Naturally, it was a done deal by the time I was asked to participate. Things have gone relatively smooth with the adoption. However, the cage is always dirty, the water bottle is always empty, and no one really ever has time to clean "Chumlee," much less visit with him. However, a recent discovery has revealed that our guinea pig has an uncontrollable appetite for carrots. The more carrots you feed him, the more carrots he wants. And the more carrots he eats, the less of the other food Chumlee desires.

The Bible clearly teaches that we all, somewhat like Chumlee, have a "flesh" that lurks about in the caves inside each of us. That "flesh" wants more and more and more when it is fed ego biscuits. Self-centeredness is part of the DNA of the flesh. The ability to arrange and order our environment to feed our self-interest is a natural instinct within every human being. Paul, the converted Saul, spoke a lot to those impulses that lie beneath the skin in man. In his epistles we are given the most detailed explanation of both "the new man in Christ" and "the old man of the flesh."

> Live freely, animated and motivated by God's Spirit. Then you won't feed the compulsions of selfishness. For there is a root of sinful self-interest in us that is at odds with a free spirit, just as the free spirit is incompatible with selfishness. These two ways of life are antithetical, so that you cannot live at times one way and at times another way according to how you feel on any given day. (Galatians 5:16-18, *The Message*)

Two questions surface regarding this flesh or the impulses of selfishness. First, does a Christian, after giving his life to Christ, still battle the flesh? And second, if we do still fight the appetites of the flesh, is it really possible to conquer sin's domination? The answer to both questions, according to the New Testament, is a double yes! Paul, in Romans 8:3-14, explained God's remedy for the limitations and sins of the flesh. God through Christ provided the Holy Spirit to believers. Now we have the real possibility of being controlled by the Spirit, not by the flesh. It is the Spirit whose life-giving power raised Jesus Christ from the dead. It is that same Spirit who can bring us life, help us grow, and give us the strength to quit feeding the flesh.

Background and upbringing

It is not automatic if you happen to be an only child, but a certain behavior pattern is called the "only child syndrome." Most of us have experienced at least one encounter with the "terrible twos" alive and well in the body of a thirty- or forty-year-old. No more diapers, no more pull-ups, but there is still a lot of mess that surrounds their people skills. This guy (let's call him Paul) actually believes the world revolves around himself. On the office wall in his mind there is a stretched map of all of the known universe. He is at the center (holding his "blankee" and bottle).

One day you meet the parents and family of Paul. All the pieces of the puzzle suddenly fall into place, and the cause of this dreadful self-centered worldview becomes clear. He was worshipped early and coddled well past the toddler years. Every time he was confronted and challenged, "Mommy made it OK," or "Daddy took care of it." He grew to become the lead part in a one-person, one-part play that ultimately becomes his program for the whole of life. This myopic, tunnel-vision kind of upbringing is difficult to shake. Some people's background makes it extremely difficult to serve others. They have no eyes to see and no ears to hear other people in the world but themselves.

CHAPTER THREE

What Serving Looks Like— Snapshots from the Bible

There is the great man who makes every man feel small, but the really great man is the man who makes every man feel great. —G.K. Chesterton[1]

The last two sections of this book are examples of serving in action. There are snapshots selected from the life and teachings of Jesus, followed by six brief vignettes from the work world. These are not to stand as the comprehensive display of servanthood but rather to stand as selected illustrations to move us beyond analysis and theory towards application.

The life and death of Jesus

If you've gotten anything at all out of following Christ, if his love has made any difference in your life, if being in a community of the Spirit means anything to you, if you have a heart, if you *care*—then do me a favor: Agree with each other, love each other, be deep-spirited friends. Don't push your way to the front; don't sweet-talk your way to the top. Put yourself aside, and help others get ahead. Don't be obsessed with getting your own advantage. Forget yourselves long enough to lend a helping hand.

Think of yourselves the way Christ Jesus thought of himself. He had equal status with God but didn't think so much of himself that he had to cling to the advantages of that status no matter what. Not at all. When the time came, he set aside the privileges of deity and took on the status of a slave, became *human!* Having become human, he stayed human. It was an incredibly humbling process. He didn't claim special privileges. Instead, he lived a selfless, obedient life and then died a selfless, obedient death—and the worst kind of death at that: a crucifixion.

Because of that obedience, God lifted him high and honored him far beyond anyone or anything, ever, so that all created beings in heaven and on earth—even those long ago dead and buried—will bow in worship before this Jesus Christ, and call out in praise that he is the Master of all, to the glorious honor of God the Father. (Philippians 2:1-11, *The Message*)

No demonstration of other-person focus will ever be greater than what Jesus Christ did. Philippians 2:1-11 gives the full story, not selected sound bites. From this historic early church hymn lay some of the most clearheaded insights on serving to ever be found.

1. *Serving can be the lowest common denominator from which to build unity into any group.*

Few things are more powerful than a well-built, truly aligned team. One way to build commonality and consensus is to ask each team member to practice at least one rule. And that rule is: Focus on the other guy, not yourself. That can form the floor for like-mindedness, one spirit, and one purpose.

2. *Serving others will always adjust our perception of ourselves.*

Real other-person focus will eventually reveal parts of us we never knew existed. When I got married, a wise elder of mine in Fort Worth, Texas, said, "Son, when you're single, you think selfishness is a two-room shack. But when you get married, you discover it is a twenty-room mansion." In other words, genuine, deep relationship with someone else will reveal compartments and closets of self-interest that we never knew we were housekeeping.

3. *Serving must always be measured against the standard of the Suffering Servant, Jesus Christ.*

This hymn records the life and status of Jesus prior to His incarnation and then follows His life through crucifixion, resurrection, and ultimately exaltation. Here are four practical insights on serving that are woven into this biography of our Lord.

a. Don't clutch too tightly the things that "rightfully" belong to you (verse 6).

b. Take on the "perspective" of the one you are trying to serve (verse 7-8).

c. Be ready for your act of serving to be unnoticed, misunderstood, or even rejected (verse 8).

d. Know that the next world, not this one, is where the serving gets rewarded (verse 9-11).

Jesus washing the disciples' feet

Jesus knew that the Father had put him in complete charge of everything, that he came from God and was on his way back to God. So he got up from the supper table, set aside his robe, and put on an apron. Then he poured water into a basin and began to wash the feet of the disciples, drying them with his apron. When he got to Simon Peter, Peter said, "Master, *you* wash *my* feet?"

Jesus answered, "You don't understand now what I'm doing, but it will be clear enough to you later."

Peter persisted, "You're not going to wash my feet—ever!"

Jesus said, "If I don't wash you, you can't be part of what I'm doing."

"Master!" said Peter. "Not only my feet, then. Wash my hands! Wash my head!"

Jesus said, "If you've had a bath in the morning, you only need your feet washed now and you're clean from head to toe. My concern, you understand, is holiness, not hygiene. So now you're clean. But not every one of you." (He knew who was betraying him. That's why he said, "Not every one of you.") After he had finished washing their feet, he took his robe, put it back on, and went back to his place at the table.

Then he said, "Do you understand what I have done to you? You address me as 'Teacher' and 'Master,' and rightly so. That is what I am. So if I, the Master and Teacher, washed your feet, you must now wash each other's feet. I've laid down a pattern for you. What I've done, you do. I'm only pointing out the obvious. A servant is not ranked about his master; an employee doesn't give orders to the employer. If you understand what I'm telling you, act like it—and live a blessed life." (John 13:3-17, *The Message*)

Jesus was entering the last fifteen to twenty hours of His life on the earth. The unmistakable lesson of this story was that Jesus wanted to take His followers back to school for a refresher course in one single area. What was it? A quick scan of all of the Old Testament personalities? No. Was it a quick review of how to preach or how to perform miracles? No. It wasn't even a review of the theology of redemption. It was a brief but never-to-be-forgotten object lesson on serving.

Why serving? Because Jesus knew serving was the motivating energy that would allow the ministry of Christ to be effectively expanded when He was gone. There would be no book of Acts without it. The disciples would never look on a foot again without noticing the dirt and thinking of Jesus. Every dirty foot could become clean, but they would have to follow the Master's model. They would have to disrobe, be willing to get a little dirty, and wring out their need to be great in the basin of cleansing service. Some additional lessons from the foot-washing demonstration are:

1. *A leader has to know what lessons are most critical to impart into his learners.*

Jesus was able to distinguish the major lessons from the minor lessons. If the leader cannot sort them correctly, there is a good chance the learner will confuse them. Servants must not confuse the strategic with the tactical, the temporal with the eternal, and thereby miss the greatest lessons connected with life.

2. *Lessons that are modeled are the most effective style of persuasion.*

I'll never forget the first time I heard Professor Howard Hendricks say it. "More is caught than taught," he thundered from the front of the classroom. No questions. We knew it was true. Case closed.

3. *Even the best students don't always connect all of the dots.*

Peter had listened, and Peter had watched. He clearly was privy to all of the before- and after-school sessions with Jesus. One could argue that no one had more of Jesus' time during the three-year school than Peter. Yet look at him here. He was still struggling to connect it all together. We should never grow discouraged or become impatient with those trying to learn the hard things of walking with Jesus. Serving others is certainly one of those hard things.

4. *Every person can become a servant.*

Washing feet was a simple act that anyone who wanted to could perform. It didn't take strength of the arms; it took strength of the heart. It didn't take brilliance. It took humility. No age restriction, no education requirements, no special lineage, just a bowl of water, a towel, and someone willing to bend his knees to care for someone else's concerns.

5. *Every person needs serving.*

There were no clean feet in the days of Jesus. Everyone who was physically able walked the dirty streets and trails in open-sandaled feet.

6. *Know-how is not always the same thing as follow-through.*

Jesus emphasized over and over to His followers: Learn it fully, then practice it completely. Whether "it" is prayer, faith, or serving other people's interest, I have to translate my know-how into a clean set of feet on the guy next to me.

The Good Samaritan

The tale of the Good Samaritan needs to be framed for best application to be gained. The road to Jericho from Jerusalem was a twisting, turning, seventeen-mile road that dropped steeply into the Jordan Valley below. There were hundreds of hidden places along the way for thieves to hide. Robberies and assault on that road were not uncommon. Priests making the trip from the Holy City, Jerusalem, weren't uncommon either. What happened to the unfortunate traveler was not at all uncommon in that day. And to that setting, add the despised half-breed Samaritan who represented a genuine racial struggle during that time, and you can really understand the parable.

"And just how would you define 'neighbor'?"

Jesus answered by telling a story.

"There was once a man traveling from Jerusalem to Jericho. On the way he was attacked by robbers. They took his clothes, beat him up, and went off leaving him half-dead. Luckily, a priest was on his way down the same road, but when he saw him he angled across to the other side. Then a Levite religious man showed up; he also avoided the injured man.

"A Samaritan traveling the road came on him. When he saw the man's condition, his heart went out to him. He gave him first aid, disinfecting and bandaging his wounds. Then he lifted him on to his donkey, led him to an inn, and made him comfortable. In the morning he took out two silver coins and gave them to the innkeeper, saying, 'Take good care of him. If it costs any more, put it on my bill—I'll pay you on my way back.'

"What do you think? Which of the three became a neighbor to the man attacked by robbers?"

"The one who treated him kindly," the religion scholar responded.

Jesus said, "Go and do the same." (Luke 10:29-37, *The Message*)

So many lessons on serving can be connected with this story.

1. *People all around us are hurting and needy.*
   a. "Stripped" of self-confidence, of self-worth, of hope, of faith, of purity, of meaning, of opportunity.
   b. "Beaten" by competition, by failure, by pressure to perform.
   c. "Abandoned," lonely, gripped by fear and doubt.
   d. Left "half dead," helpless, and hopeless.

2. *We can avoid serving, even in the name of religion.*
   Two religious professionals walked by the wounded neighbor. As a matter of fact, they even altered their course to "the other side" so as to eliminate contact and possible confrontation. Religious busyness often tramples right over human need.

Formalism, ritualism, and institutionalism can drive religious machinery right over hurting, needy people, all in the name of religion itself.

3. *Serving requires deliberate actions for any result to occur.*
   a. It takes initiative. The Samaritan took a relational chance. He knew he was hated and disliked, but he risked anyway.
   b. It takes adjustment. The Samaritan obviously was going somewhere himself. I doubt seriously his Franklin or Day-Timer had filled in for that day: Tuesday, May 15, 11:00 to 2:00, "Roam around road to Jericho looking for assault victims to help."

For years I thought the Samaritan was a full-time, two-donkey traveling medical unit. Not at all. He obviously missed his appointment and had his schedule wrecked that day. Effective serving sometimes results in that.

   c. It takes sacrifice. The Samaritan gave time. He gave money. He gave compassion. He obviously got his hands dirty helping to clean up the stripped, beaten man.

d. It takes sensitivity. The story clearly identifies the Samaritan as "seeing" or "spotting" the wounded man. Serving others always begins with being able to spot and recognize a person who could use a little help.

Early in this book we defined serving as the art and act of focusing on someone else's interest instead of my own. The Bible is full of stories that illustrate this life message. For example, David, Daniel, Nehemiah, and Joseph all evidenced early in their lives a servant's heart and a servant's actions. And undoubtedly, serving others was one of the predominant themes of the life of Jesus. It is impossible to read any significant section of Scripture and not see the strong serving theme in God's message to man.

CHAPTER FOUR

What Serving Looks Like— Snapshots from Life

A Christian man is a perfectly free lord of all, subject to none. A Christian man is a perfectly dutiful servant, subject to all. —Martin Luther[1]

(*Author's Note:* When we asked Christians to talk about how they serve others in the workplace, a dilemma developed. Because we picked people we knew had shown a passion for serving others, all were willing and eager to help. But the focus of their serving always has been on God, and none of them were eager to direct attention to themselves. The last thing any of us wanted was self-serving stories about serving. In looking for illustrations for this series, the topic was easily the most sensitive. So, while the content and examples in the following stories are accurate, the names of the people and their companies have been changed.)

Serving your employees

Andrew Colston

Sometimes the most elemental of solutions are the ones that get overlooked in the high-speed culture of modern corporate America. Complex problems require complex solutions, don't they? If the question isn't simple, how simple can the answer be?

But when Andrew Colston approaches the daunting task of serving his employees, he begins with the most basic, and simplest, of foundations: prayer.

Andrew, the president and founder of a successful retail business, has around two hundred employees. And every morning before reporting to work, the man at the top of their corporate ladder gets down on his knees and prays for them.

Andrew, whose wife often joins him in prayer, asks God to bless his employees and make them happy and also productive in their work. If they are happy, Andrew knows they will be productive. If they are productive, Andrew knows they will be happy.

But Andrew also can be specific in his prayers. He isn't able to pray for every employee every day. But over the course of time, he works his way through the entire company—name by name, need by need. Then he starts over again.

The employees, of course, benefit from the prayers, even though most of them never know that their boss has lifted them up.

The process also prepares Andrew for his day at the office. He arrives not as a detached corporate executive who ascends to an isolated ivory tower but as a man who is sensitized to the needs of the people who work for him. He becomes challenged to find out more and more about each employee, which allows him to serve their complex needs in any number of simple ways—the first, of course, being prayer.

Andrew Colston's prayers aren't always answered the way he would like. And the ones that are answered aren't always answered on his timetable.

But Paul Lee, for one, is grateful that Andrew never let such frustrations stop him from modeling the Christian life.

Paul has worked for Andrew for more than twenty-six years, but it was only recently that he came to know Christ. For years, Andrew has patiently modeled the gospel in the workplace, hoping and praying that it would have an impact on people such as Paul. In time, it did. Andrew doesn't try to convert anyone by force, which is one of the things Paul appreciates most about his boss. Paul wasn't won over through "gorilla evangelism," but because each day he sees leadership by example. He sees a man who always is available, a man who listens, and a man who cares. He sees a man who looks for solutions without placing blame, a man who always sees more in other people than those people see in themselves. He sees a man who leads with his heart and his soul, not with selfish impulses. And he sees a man who is rewarded for his lifestyle.

Through the years, Andrew's leadership has produced a company that is known as much for its integrity as its profitability. And in the process, he has served as a personal beam of light that eventually has led many around him, like Paul, out of the darkness.

STAN MORRIS

When the National Collegiate Athletic Association's main office in Kansas City was at its bureaucratic worst, employees were considered tardy if they arrived after 8:30 a.m.

Their thermal drapes had to be pulled, their desks had to be cleared at the end of each day, and no day would end prior to 5 p.m. Every employee worked every other Saturday and adhered to a strict dress code. And no one took a coffee break or was allowed to even bring a drink of any sort to their desk.

There was even a manual—NCAA Office Policies and Procedures—that was more than a hundred pages of rules for the workplace.

It was, one would imagine, about as opposite as any business could be run from the small but profitable company Stan Morris's family has operated for three generations.

Stan has his own dress code: Everyone has to come to work dressed. He has rules about the hours his thirteen employees keep: Be here when you are supposed to be here unless you need to be somewhere else. And the only clock his employees punch is the one that wakes them up each morning.

Stan believes he best serves his employees by treating them like family. That doesn't mean they sleep at his house, eat his food, and ask his wife to wash their laundry. But it does mean they can expect a certain leeway when a request is legitimate (and maybe an occasional cookout).

All Stan asks for in return is that they treat him and his company the same way—like it is part of their family.

Stan realizes this approach is only as good as the people he hires. But, so far, it has worked to the betterment of everyone involved.

Members of Stan's support staff are allowed to take off if their kids have doctor's appointments or school functions. But they willingly come in early or work through their lunch hour to make up the time. And because Stan serves them by providing flexible hours—a privilege they would like to keep—they serve each other by picking up the slack for anyone who needs it.

There have been those who abuse the system, of course. But Stan sees the silver lining there, as well. Take, for instance, the man he hired who spent most of his days in the back room working his own multilevel market interest. Stan was aware of the problem, but, as usual, he was willing to give the guy a second chance. So he headed to the back room to suggest that the employee spend less time making personal calls and more time representing the person who was providing the office and the company car.

But before he could get the words out of his mouth, the man announced that he had been offered a coaching job in a neighboring state and that he planned to accept the position.

The way Stan sees it, God took care of the problem. And even though the man had cost the company money, Stan felt blessed by the opportunity to see God's hand work in the situation. It was an opportunity that might never have come if he had been following some hundred-page manual.

Serving your staff

JIM ALLEN

Jim Allen's vocation is all about serving others, but this pastor of a growing Bible church realizes there is a tendency to overlook the people who are paid to serve him.

It is a common pitfall for busy bosses. They are eager to serve their clients, customers, or, in this case, parishioners, but in doing so, they ignore the needs of their hardworking staff. They become blinded to the needs of the people they are in the best position to serve.

Jim tries to avoid this pitfall by practicing what he calls "water-fountain management." It is his mechanism for building relationships with the people who work in his church. Jim spends as much time as possible visiting with the people on his staff, learning their strengths and weaknesses, their hopes and their dreams, their problems and their victories.

Jim can be an extremely task-focused individual, and there are times when that is an extremely important aspect of his job. But for brief stretches of time each day, he turns off that side of his personality and turns on the relationship-focused side.

He visits the water fountain.

The knowledge Jim drinks in from around "the water fountain" helps him know and serve the needs of his staff. If he knows a person's strengths, he can hold that person accountable so that those strengths don't grow out of control. If he knows a person's weaknesses, he can offer encouragement or practical advice to help build them up.

If he knows their needs, he is more likely to meet their needs.

That is why he offered a hand to the building superintendent when it came time to lift a new wall for an addition to the church office. Jim didn't wait to find out about the man's back problem by hearing a scream of agony from a guy with a wrenched muscle. Instead, he already knew the man didn't need to do any heavy lifting. He had learned that information weeks earlier during one of their regular chats; then Jim had stored the information away. Now he was there to serve this staff member in a very practical way. In doing so, Jim lifted not only the wall but also the man standing beside him.

Serving your patients

CLIFF IVERS

Cliff Ivers doesn't like going to the dentist, which is one of the big reasons why he is such a patient-friendly dentist himself.

Cliff tries to operate his practice by adhering to a modified version of the Golden Rule: Treat your patients the way you would want to be treated if you were the patient. It is a philosophy that works particularly well for a man who would much rather be standing beside the chair than sitting in it.

When his patients sit down, Cliff wants them to know that he has been there before, that he knows what it is like, and that he will do everything within his power to make the experience as pleasant as possible.

He keeps a twinkle in his eyes, a smile on his face, and good humor in his voice, even on the days when he feels his worst.

But Cliff's style requires more than a comforting chair-side manner.

Cliff tries to view his entire work world through the patient's eyes. What do they see when they come through the door? How does everything from the wallpaper to the magazines to the staff work to affect the patient's mood? All of these things are important parts of Cliff's goal of serving his patients.

He doesn't want his practice to become assembly-line dentistry with a "drill 'em, fill 'em, and bill 'em" mentality. He's committed to something much more personal, and that commitment extends to every aspect of his office.

Cliff makes a deliberate attempt to create an office style and culture around him that is friendly to his patients. That means he has to be upbeat and encouraging. And that means he has to find ways to reward his staff for following suit. It means spending a little extra on incentive programs for his staff. It means reinvesting profits back into people and systems. Recently, Cliff bought a new piece of equipment that costs more than either of his automobiles. He thought he would never get over the sticker shock. And it means spending a little extra to keep the office decor fresh and up-to-date.

In short, it means doing whatever it takes to satisfy and serve the most cranky patient Cliff could encounter—himself.

Serving your boss

TED MELVIN

If Ted Melvin's boss can order from a menu, then the senior executive of a Fortune 25 company should survive just fine.

As the director of purchasing and one of eight direct reports to one of the company's senior executives, Ted wants to carry out his duties so that his boss has only two major concerns—what to eat and what to drink. Everything else he can leave to Ted.

It is an approach Ted has taken from the biblical life of Joseph. The Old Testament says Joseph served Potiphar to such a degree that all Potiphar had to worry about was what he would eat and what he would drink. Everything else he put in Joseph's charge; Potiphar did not concern himself with it anymore.

The simple principle is the driving force behind Ted's philosophy of servanthood in the workplace. He never wants his boss to worry about anything that Ted is in charge of carrying out. When Ted is given an assignment, he doesn't want his boss to think about it again until complete and competent results have been delivered—ahead of schedule.

This philosophy serves Ted's boss well because it allows him to focus on other issues. It serves Ted well in a spiritual sense because it is biblically sound, and it serves him well in a secular sense because it earns him the respect and admiration of his boss. And since he models the philosophy well for the people who report to him, it serves others well. It touches people above, below, and all around him.

Ted proves his value to his boss again and again. And Ted's charges learn to show their value to Ted again and again. In turn, everyone in the loop becomes valuable to the organization. And when their work is done, all they need to think about is what to eat and what to drink.

Serving peers and coworkers

EDWARD MARVIN

Keeping a watchful eye on his fellow pilots had become second nature for Edward, just as it had become second nature for his fellow pilots to keep an eye on him.

They all knew the demands of their job as pilots for an international missionary ministry, and an instinctive bond had developed between the members of the team. They were there to take care of each other, to make each other better, and to keep the entire crew flying with maximum productivity. The result was that each of the individual parts became stronger than it ever could be alone.

That is why Edward hardly gave a second thought to the idea of flying every day for three straight weeks so that the pilots who needed a rest could get it. He just did it. And that is why the pilots who needed a break hardly gave a second thought to allowing Edward to take some of their flights.

They would do, and often did, the exact same thing for him. It was that way for Edward's twelve years as a pilot for this ministry, and it was that way during his yearlong stint as an aviator during Vietnam.

The culture of serving one's peers was intentionally cultivated and grown by these men until its roots dug deep into their very souls. And it is a culture Edward has carried with him into the corporate world at every stop in his career.

To Edward, serving a fellow airman by taking one of his flights is no different than spending time with a new employee to make sure his adjustment to the job goes smoothly. That person eventually would become acclimated to the new environment, just as the other pilots would make their scheduled trips even if they were tired.

But in both cases, the whole process went more smoothly with a little extra effort—effort that was unsolicited and unrewarded in secular terms—from someone willing to serve.

It is a type of spiritually based leadership, one that follows the example set by Jesus and one that others often adopt and spread to those around them until pretty soon no one is really sure who is leading this call to servanthood. But they all know they are better off because it is there.

Serving clients

TIM DAILEY

The family business began back in 1879, and sometime during the second generation's proprietorship, a company motto was established.

It was a simple four-word credo: Service beyond the contract.

It sounded good, and Tim, the third-generation owner and president, has no reason to believe there was anything cosmetic about the stance his father had proclaimed for the business. But since his father, like his grandfather, wasn't a Christian, Tim knows the attraction to a biblically supported philosophy was purely coincidental.

For Tim, however, the motto is much more than something he stamps on his stationery or pastes in bold letters across the company's ad in the yellow pages. It is a way of life.

Tim sees it as part of his Christian obligation to live out that motto of service to his customers, even if it isn't always the most profitable avenue to take.

As president of an independent insurance agency, Tim knows he is in an industry that often pays lip service to such flashy mottoes.

Not Tim.

Whenever a customer's policy is due for renewal, Tim always includes a personal letter that outlines the coverage the policyholder has and the options available for the renewal. Many times, these options lower both the premium for the customer and the commission for Tim's agency.

When a car reaches the age where comprehensive and collision coverages no longer are cost-effective, Tim is the first one to tell the customer that such coverages should be dropped.

Tim wants to show a personal interest in the assets of his customers. He wants them to know that he treasures their treasures. And he wants them to know he is recommending to them the very same coverage he would purchase for himself if he were in their shoes.

Truly living the company's motto sometimes cost the business money in the short run. But it is also an investment. Tim knows that nine out of every ten customers he has renew with his agency, even when sometimes he is unable to beat a competitor's price.

The personal relationship he builds creates the type of loyalty that led one commercial customer to stay with Tim's firm even though his best offer was $6,000 higher than a competitor.

Tim's father and grandfather no doubt saw the business sense in building strong relationships with customers—of offering service beyond the contract. But Tim sees the spiritual sense. To him, service isn't so much an extension of the contract as it is a part of the contract—not the one his customer signed with his agency, but one Jesus signed with His blood.

Conclusion

Anyway

People are unreasonable, illogical, and self-centered,
    Love them anyway.
If you do good, people will accuse you of selfish, ulterior
motives,
    Do good anyway.
If you are successful, you win false friends and true enemies,
    Succeed anyway.
The good you do will be forgotten tomorrow,
    Do good anyway.
Honesty and frankness make you vulnerable,
    Be honest and frank anyway.
What you spent years building may be destroyed overnight,
    Build anyway.
People really need help but may attack you if you help them,
    Help people anyway.

Give the world the best you have and you will get kicked
in the teeth,
    Give the world the best you've got anyway.
        —From a sign on the wall of Shishu Bhavan,
        the children's home in Calcutta

Where Do I Go from Here?

1. *Memorize.*

   Memorize Mark 10:43-45 and the working definition of serving mentioned in the front of this book.

2. *Audit.*

   Perform a 360-degree servanthood audit on yourself. Ask those who work over you, under you, and next to you for some feedback on their perception of your "servant performance."

3. *Pray.*

   List three people in your work environment, and begin praying every day for them. Pray for their success, growth, and advancement.

4. *Lead.*

   Take fifteen minutes on serving, and lead your family through a devotional on serving others. This will help you to better personalize the servant concepts as well as educate your family towards other people.

5. *Draft.*

   Write out a vision statement for your performance at work that is clearly built around your helping other people achieve, attain, and accomplish. Post it.

Notes

Chapter One

1. Edythe Draper, *Draper's Book of Quotations for the Christian World* (Wheaton, Ill.: Tyndale House Publishers, Inc., 1992), p. 555.
2. Robert K. Greenleaf, *On Becoming a Servant-Leader,* ed. Don M. Frick and Larry C. Spears (New York: Paulist Press, 1977), p. 31.

Chapter Two

1. Edythe Draper, *Draper's Book of Quotations for the Christian World* (Wheaton, Ill.: Tyndale House Publishers, Inc., 1992), p. 562.
2. Robert N. Bellah et al., *Habits of the Heart,* Perennial Library edition (New York: Harper & Row, 1985), p. vii.

Chapter Three

1. Edythe Draper, *Draper's Book of Quotations for the Christian World* (Wheaton, Ill.: Tyndale House Publishers, Inc., 1992), p. 286.

Chapter Four

1. John Blanchard, *More Gathered Gold—A Treasury of Quotations for Christmas* (Nappanee, Ind.: Evangelical Press, 1986), p. 38.

If you liked this book and would like to know more
about ™Life@WorkCo.™ or Cornerstone, please call us
at 1-800-739-7863.

Other ways to reach us:

Mail: Post Office Box 1928
          Fayetteville, AR 72702

Fax: (501) 443-4125

E-mail: LifeWork@CornerstoneCo.com